To Joseph Rodota

THE BEEFEATERS
OF THE
TOWER OF LONDON

With best wishes

from one of your

'subjects' !!

Thank you for an excellent
portrait.

from the authors

J. Abbott
and Shelagh Abbott.

14 May 1987

THE
BEEFEATERS
OF THE
TOWER OF
LONDON

G. Abbott

Yeoman Warder (retd)
HM Tower of London
Member of Her Majesty's Bodyguard of the
Yeomen of the Guard Extraordinary

Verses
by
Shelagh Abbott

DAVID & CHARLES
Newton Abbot London North Pomfret (Vt)

Dedicated to my colleagues, the Yeoman Warders
of Her Majesty's Tower of London, not forgetting
the multitude of visitors whose questions inspired
this book

British Library Cataloguing in Publication Data

Abbott, G.
    The Beefeaters of the Tower of London.
    1.   Tower of London——History
    I.   Title
    942.1'5   DA687.T7

    ISBN   0–7153–8636–0

Photoset by Photo-graphics, Honiton
and printed in Great Britain
by Billings, Worcester
for David & Charles (Publishers) Limited
Brunel House   Newton Abbot   Devon

Published in the United States of America
by David & Charles Inc
North Pomfret   Vermont 05053   USA

Contents

Introduction

We are not film extras or fancy dress salesmen.
We do not commute to work in the Tower each day and
    travel home in the evening.
We do not wear 'costumes'.
We do not have to grow a beard.
We are not compelled to smile into tourists' cameras.
We do not inherit the job from our ancestors.
We are not even 'Beefeaters' – or 'Buffetiers'!
So what are we?

We are the Yeoman Warders and our homes are in Her Majesty's
Tower of London. Our pictures appear in books and magazines,
on posters, postcards and brochures, in newspapers and on the
television, worldwide.

The two and a half million or more visitors who come to the
Tower each year see us on duty within the grounds. We marshal
the queues, assist the bewildered and guide the foreigners, most
of us being able to nod in Spanish and point in Japanese.

We are ever watchful for those of evil intent, be they terrorist or
pickpocket. We help the lost and the sick, we joke with the
cheerful and give sweets to the tearful. No family album is
apparently complete without a snap of one of us with the
children, and no holiday video is worth showing to the folks back
home if it doesn't include a real live chat with a yeoman warder.

We try to ensure that the tourists, despite their jetlag, aching
feet, the crowds and the weather, still enjoy their visit to the
Tower. We may finish up exhausted – but we do try! And even
after the curfew bell has ushered out the last lingering tourist of
the day, our duties still continue. For the Royal Palace and
Fortress must be guarded as it has always been for over nine
hundred years, by the yeoman warders.

Our story has never been told before, and I hope to answer the
many questions posed by our friends, the visitors, and to describe
our traditions and way of life here in the Tower of London.

1 The Early Days

If there would be a sight for all to look upon
And say 'This, then, is Britain!'
For sensibility's sake let there be chosen
  A Yeoman Warder.
Set him to stand athwart our heritage,
For none is more proud of it.
Approve his service,
For none is more honourable.
Place him in cloth of scarlet well adorned with gold,
And ye shall in him our very nation thus behold.

More than nine hundred years ago a castle was built, bigger, more substantial than any ever seen before in this country. Because of its impregnable strength and strategic position, the royal families lived there amid the glitter and ceremony of the royal court for nearly six centuries. The castle provided safe-keeping for the treasures of the realm and the gold coins of the Mint; it housed the courts of justice and the nation's armoury; and it held secure the king's enemies and state prisoners.

The castle was, of course, Her Majesty's Tower of London, still a royal palace and fortress, and those who have guarded its noble residents and priceless treasures since the eleventh century are now known as Yeoman Warders, and erroneously as the Beefeaters! In effect, they lined history's route, watching – and guarding – the cavalcade of the high and mighty, the doomed and the damned, who passed through the Tower's portals, from the little princes to Sir Walter Raleigh, Anne Boleyn to Sir Thomas More, and Guy Fawkes to Rudolf Hess.

In their early days the yeoman warders were known as Yeomen of the Crown, a yeoman being an officer or office holder of the Court; and although their title has changed through the ages, this body of royal retainers has true claim to being the oldest of any known association of men carrying on

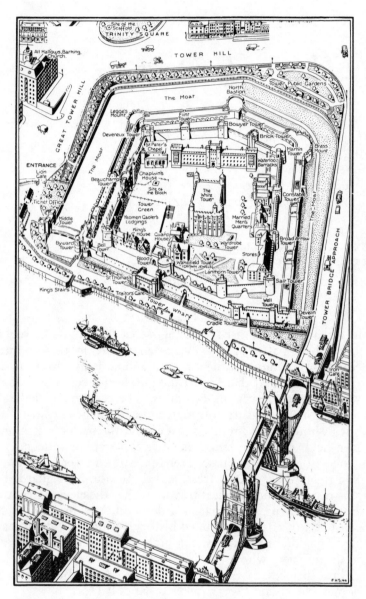

Map of the Tower of London c1910

the same duties from century to century.

One vitally important duty was, and still is, the securing of the entrances to the Tower, and in 1321 John of London was employed 'to open the main gates and lock them at the usual hours, to shake the bars and search the locks, then deliver the keys to the Lieutenant of the Tower. For that he would receive fourpence per day, a Rugg Gown [red coat], and halbert as the rest of the yeomen had' (Warders Order Book). And doubtless it was another yeoman who earned the reward bestowed by Henry VII: 'Grant for life to Robert Jay, in consideration of his true service within this our Realm, of the keeping of our new bulwark at our Tower of London, with the house upon the Tower Wharf and the gardens upon Tower Hill, with all wages, fees etc. to such keeping pertaining' (State Papers, Henry VII). Other duties included attendance at coronations and royal funerals, and guarding the prisoners and treasures – of which more will be explained in later chapters.

A command structure for these Tower guardians was necessary, and so supervisory posts of Yeoman Porter and Yeoman Gaoler were eventually created. The latter had responsibility for the thousands of prisoners who, over the centuries, were confined in the Tower; while the Yeoman Porter concerned himself with the security of the entrances to the Tower – a vital task indeed, involving not only the gates, but the drawbridges and portcullises.

Three drawbridges protected the main entrance, and needless to say had to be maintained in good order. The outermost one was positioned just inside the present gates, and the slots in which the drawbridge counterweights swung are still visible in the pit there. The next one, long gone, barred the approach to the Middle Tower, a bastion which was virtually an island in the moat. A further one linked Middle to Byward Tower, the entrance proper to the fortress. Other smaller drawbridges gave access from the Wharf at different stages in the Tower's development.

Drawbridges had slots and so did the portcullises, those for the latter being situated within many archways, vertically down each wall. Under threat of attack, the portcullises, heavy sliding doors or gratings, would be lowered, the spikes on their bases sinking into the ground to resist battering. The grooves in the walls effectively prevented the use of levers, and as further deterrents, defenders could fire arrows through the slits strategically sited each side of the archway and pour oil or scalding water down on to their attackers' heads through three large holes above.

Most archways were equipped with two portcullises, one on each side of the great doors, and the Byward and Bloody Towers still retain one in their arches, with the necessary hoisting mechanism above. The small hole in the surviving Byward portcullis was for the benefit of a retreating defender left outside the tower, or for the admittance of an emissary seeking a truce. It is not much larger than a porthole and can only be passed through with difficulty, head first, ensuring that anyone entering had to have extremely friendly intentions or a very hard head! This hole, unobserved by the millions of tourists passing beneath it each year, is just visible above the menacing spikes. If the portcullis was kept permanently lowered, the use of the hole would make the collection of admission tickets considerably easier!

The doors themselves are no flimsy barrier and, like the hole in the portcullis, the small posterns in the main doors are only big enough to admit one person at a time, with difficulty.

In 1509 an event occurred which gave the Tower guardians a new identity. Henry VII had just died, and his young son Henry VIII retired to the Tower to mourn in private and doubtless to plan his future. He was accompanied by some of his Bodyguard of the Yeomen of the Guard, a body of men instituted by his father in 1485. After a decent interval, he moved out of the Tower but left behind fifteen of his bodyguard. These, together with those who had already guarded both royalty and the Tower for four centuries, became a distinct corps known in the Payments as Yeomen of the Tower.

In 1550 the Duke of Somerset received such considerate treatment as a prisoner that, when pardoned, he asked the king, Edward VI, to grant the warders the right to wear the uniform of the Yeomen of the Guard. This was done, with the exception of the crossbelt supporting the carbine or arquebus, the warders not needing such a weapon and having been formed long before firearms were invented anyway.

As an indication of the importance of their duties, a royal decree of 1572 warned the warders that 'they were not to leave the Tower without permission, upon pain of forfeiture of 12 pence [5p] for the first default, and the second default 3 shillings [15p]; the third default, his body to be imprisoned three days, and if he makes default the fourth time, to lose his room for ever, and his body to be punished at the King's pleasure'. A further regulation in 1608, bearing the sign-manual of James I, described the warders' tasks more fully: 'that 25 warders shall always remain within the Tower, to guard and attend to the keeping of the gates from their first opening in the morning until closing at night, and that each warder shall bear in his hands a halbert or bill wheresoever they go within the said Tower.'

The title of Yeomen of the Tower changed with the passing of time. In 1685 they were known as 'Yeomen of the Guard, Warders of the Tower' and this eventually diminished to 'Tower Warders'. Now, their proud title in full is 'Yeoman Warders of Her Majesty's Royal Palace and Fortress the Tower of London, Members of the Sovereign's Bodyguard of the Yeomen of the Guard Extraordinary'. The latter distinction carries with it the requirement to reinforce the Yeomen of the Guard in Ordinary whenever necessary.

The warders are almost invariably referred to as the 'Beefeaters'. As this nickname was applied to them as early as the seventeenth century, there is little point in further protests, though by rights it belongs to the Yeomen of the Guard in Ordinary, not the yeoman warders. The origin of the nickname is not known, and guesses connecting the word with food tasters called buffetiers are erroneous, there being no such word in the French language.

Yet another plausible derivation alleges that, as members of the royal bodyguard, they were permitted to eat as much beef as they wished from the king's table and then to take away as much as they could carry on their daggers, for their families. Support for this is quoted in Queen Elizabeth's Household Book for the year 1601. Referring to her food servers, it states: 'the Yeomen of the Mouth to have 100 shillings [£5] a-yeere a-peece, also two messes of meate of three dishes a-peece allowed for them and the rest of the Officers of the Pantry.'

The confusion as to who are the Beefeaters was made worse by Gilbert and Sullivan in their operetta *Yeomen of the Guard*. The story unfolds within the Tower and involves the warders, and so the correct title should have been 'The Tower Warders'. In fact the composers had them sing:

Tower Warders, under orders, gallant pikemen, valiant sworders,

2 The Officers and Their Men

At the head of their men
And the feet of their Queen
These military leaders
Together are seen
Trimming the lamp
Of loyalty yet
Lest any amongst us
Should chance to forget
The might of his country
The fame and the power
That billoweth yet
From the heart of the Tower.

The Constable

Traditionally, the man who held the Tower controlled London, and he who held London controlled England. So whenever the king left the Tower to visit his domains or lead his army abroad, he had to ensure that the Tower remained in the charge of a man possessing the highest integrity and loyalty. Many an absent baron lost his stronghold while his back was turned, and similarly a monarch dared not risk his kingdom to a rival.

The Constable of the Tower, for he it is who commands the fortress on behalf of the sovereign, holds one of the highest offices in the land, and one that has continued almost unbroken since Geoffrey de Mandeville, a Norman knight, was appointed in 1078. Various titles have been used over the centuries – Constable of London, Constable of the Honour of the Tower – and because the fortress is still a royal palace, the Constable has the right and privilege of audience and direct communication with his monarch. He holds his appointment by Royal Letters-

Patent under the Great Seal; it was originally for life but nowadays the installation of a new Constable takes place every five years, the impressive ceremony being described in a later chapter.

The earlier Constables were, of course, Norman knights, and in 1214 Prince Louis of France was entrusted with the task. Several others were bishops, men of great learning who, through their studies, excelled in military strategy – indeed, the Tower itself was designed by a monk, Gundulf of Bec, in Normandy.

Despite the high qualifications required, it is hardly surprising that of the 154 Constables who have served since the eleventh century, a few failed to set a good example to their yeoman warders. One was another Geoffrey de Mandeville, Constable in 1140 and grandson of the first Constable. This turbulent knight eventually rebelled against the king and became the leader of a band of highwaymen and robbers. Plundering rich merchants and richer abbeys, he was finally cornered by King Stephen's troops. During the battle he took off his helmet because of the heat, whereupon an arrow pierced his brain and killed him. As he had been excommunicated by the Pope for his sacrilegious robberies, his followers dared not bury him, but some Knights Templar took his body to London. They wrapped it in a leaden sheet and suspended it from a tree in the grounds of the Temple. And there it swayed for twenty years until Pope Alexander III lifted the ban, allowing the remains to be buried near the west door of Temple Church and a stone effigy of de Mandeville to be placed within.

The next Constable to meet an unpleasant end was Bishop Stapleton. He fell foul of the Londoners, and on 14 October 1326 his house was ransacked and he was caught near St Paul's Cathedral. The mob, howling for his blood, dragged him to Cheapside. There, accused of being a traitor and a destroyer of their liberties, he was executed, his head being stuck on a pole on London Bridge.

In 1446 John Holland, Duke of Exeter, was appointed Constable, and in his memory a magnificent effigy lies within the Chapel Royal of St Peter ad Vincula. A less pleasant monument was employed for many years in the deepest vaults of the White Tower, for Holland is believed responsible for introducing the dreaded rack into this country from the Continent. This instrument of torture consists of a long rectangular frame with a roller at each end to which the victim's limbs were

The Staff of the Constable of the Tower

tied. Rotating the rollers pulled him – or her – clear of the floor, causing excruciating pain and dislocation of the joints. Being so cruelly maltreated was known with grim jocularity as 'being wedded to the Duke of Exeter's Daughter', an alliance from which an early divorce was eagerly sought.

A few years later, in 1461, John Tipcroft, Earl of Worcester, became Constable, but within nine years a charge of treason was levied against him. He was taken to Tower Hill, overlooking the castle he once commanded, and his head was cut off and paraded through the City.

These gentlemen were of course the exceptions, and even their crimes were, in many cases, political offences. For the last 250 years the appointment of Constable has been granted to soldiers of high distinction – field marshals and generals with outstanding military records.

In the early days the Constable's income of £100 a year was considerably augmented by perquisites from numerous sources. He received fees from the prisoners 'for the sute of their yrons': for a duke £20, an earl £15, a baron £10 and a knight £5. These fees came from the prisoners' goods and estates seized by the Treasury, who also paid for the prisoner's board, coal and candle during his sentence. Should the prisoner through pride or contempt refuse that allowance, it too passed to the Constable. It was truly said that only rich men could afford to be captive in the Tower!

Nor by any means was the Constable's income limited by the Tower's walls. He received rents for the tenements and herb gardens on Tower Hill and a tenth of the profit made by those who dried skins in East Smithfield. The moat itself was a great source of money, for owners of horses and cattle caught grazing on its sloping banks were fined 1d a hoof, 4d per beast, and every cart which slithered into its muddy depths became the Constable's property.

The river between London Bridge and the Tower yielded a rich harvest. All flotsam and jetsam were his, and all swans floating downriver made their appetising appearance later, on his banqueting table. Animals falling off the bridge, and fish caught from the Wharf also filled his larders, together with one basketful from the cargo of all boats laden with oysters, mussels and cockles.

Lavish meals thus provided would have been unpalatable without wine, and the Constable was never short of that. Ships bringing wine from Bordeaux had to hand over two flagons, one from before and the other from aft of the mast, and from each galley he collected two roundletts (a measure quoted in a document of Richard II in 1381) of wine and a quantity of dainties. The wine was placed in the care of the Keeper of the Tower Bottles. From 1609 to 1619 the Keeper was a man called Taylor, who maintained two bottles or bombards of leather, each of three gallons capacity. These were stored in the cellars of the Lieutenant's Lodgings (renamed the King's or Queen's House, as appropriate, after 1880) within the Tower, and replenished from passing ships when necessary.

Just as German castles built on islands in the River Rhine exacted tolls from river craft before allowing them to continue their journey, so the Tower's commanding position on London's river brought the same advantage. Herring boats from Yarmouth had to pay 12d (5p) each boat, and others fishing for sprats paid 8s (40p) a year, though if they were based in London, only 6s 8d (33p) was demanded. Foreign merchants bringing herrings paid 8s, and any cargo thrown overboard from vessels in trouble belonged to the Constable, as did any ship over 6 tons deserted by its crew, though he did allow its owner to buy it back from him! Half the goods brought ashore without the customs having been paid were handed over, and for some strange though doubtless lucrative reason, the Constable collected 2d (1p) from every person going on or returning from a pilgrimage by river to the Shrine of St James of Compostella.

All this river traffic was signalled to anchor and pay the dues by the Yeoman Porter or his deputy who, standing on Tower Wharf or the battlements, would hold up a staff of office, one of which still survives in the Tower. Over 3ft (91cm) long and of dark wood, it is twisted throughout its length like a giant corkscrew; on its short handle is a brass plate bearing the inscription 'Tower 1671'.

Ships of foreign navies visiting the City usually moored near London Bridge, and their captains lost no time in coming to the Tower to assure the Constable or his representative of the ship's peaceful intentions towards the capital. The practice is continued to this very day. NATO and other warship captains still pay visits to the Queen's House on arrival, though hardly intimidated by the rows of ancient cannon along the Wharf!

The Lieutenant

In Elizabethan times the living conditions in the Tower had become so squalid and plague-ridden that the Constable moved out, though retaining his pay and perquisites. The operational command of the fortress, on a day-to-day basis, was then handed over to his deputy, the Lieutenant of the Tower.

Noblemen or high-ranking officers appointed as Lieutenant were first recorded in 1189, and had previously commanded the Tower during temporary absences of the Constable. Their qualifications were of the same exemplary standard as those of the Constable, absolute dedication and loyalty being demanded. Most of them lived through exciting times in the Tower, playing leading roles in such dramas as Raleigh's long imprisonment, the disappearance of the little princes, Sir Thomas More's harsh confinement and Lady Jane Grey's tragic death.

Two sixteenth-century Lieutenants, father and son, lie buried in the Chapel Royal of St Peter ad Vincula. Their handsomely carved marble monument contains two skulls: one of alabaster and the other belonging to either Sir Richard or Sir Michael Blount. Another monument in the chapel is surmounted by the superb effigies of Sir Richard Cholmondeley and his wife Elizabeth. He was Lieutenant of the Tower in the reign of

Henry VIII and had the monument carved before his death, doubtless so that he could admire it while sitting in his official pew during church services. Unfortunately, in 1518, a riot broke out between the Londoners and foreign merchants. Cholmondeley, in modern parlance, overreacted, ordering his new cannon on the battlements to open fire, or as phrased at the time, 'Chomley, no great frende to the citie, in a frantyke fury, losed certayn peces of ordinance and shot into the citie, which did little harm, but his good wyll disapeered' (Sutherland Gower, page 41).

Dismissed from his post, Cholmondeley eventually died and was buried elsewhere, and when the tomb was opened during the restoration of the chapel in December 1876, all that it contained were large fragments of stone. These pieces were carefully reassembled to form the ancient Tudor font which now stands within the chapel and is used for the baptism of children of the yeoman warders. It is believed that the font was hidden there by a priest in Cromwell's time, to prevent it being destroyed like so many of the Tower's other valuables. The priest is thought to have been killed by the Roundheads, and so the tomb kept its secret for two centuries or more.

Cholmondeley's successor was Sir Leonard Skeffington, a gentleman who had obviously studied the rack in the White Tower very closely. Realising that it persuaded by stretching, he went to the other extreme and invented a device which did almost the opposite. The victim, doubled up, was encircled by a wide hinged hoop which was then slowly tightened by screws until the blood spurted and death by crushing resulted. And just as the rack became known as 'the Duke of Exeter's Daughter', so this machine was given the name 'Skeffington's Daughter', which changed by usage to 'the Scavenger's Daughter'. Whether instruments such as this were operated by the yeoman warders is open to doubt, but as torture was not legal, there was no official position like that of executioner or hangman.

Monuments, effigies and instruments of torture are all visible mementoes of past Lieutenants, unlike that of Sir John Barkstead, who is believed to have buried treasure in the Tower during his term of office. Originally a goldsmith in the Strand, he became one of Cromwell's Roundhead officers and went on to achieve prominence as Governor of Reading and Member of Parliament for Colchester. Later, as a judge, he participated in the trial of Charles I which resulted in the execution of that noble monarch. In 1652, Barkstead commanded the Tower as its Lieutenant and was knighted after four years. The pickings in the Tower at that time were particularly good, the state prison being full of Royalist and other prisoners, and Barkstead wasted no time in extorting a vast amount of money from his hapless charges.

After the Restoration of the Monarchy in 1660, however, the harvest came to an abrupt end and Barkstead fled to the Continent, abandoning, some said, over £7,000 in gold, packed in butter firkins and buried within the grounds. He settled in Germany and, lulled into complacency, later paid a visit to friends in Holland. But the king's spies were everywhere, and this news reached the ears of the king's agent in the Netherlands, Sir George Downing (after whom the street was named). Barkstead was captured and brought to England. After his trial by the Royalists, he was executed at Tyburn on 19 April 1662, his quarters being placed on various of the City's gates. It is reported that his severed head was stuck on a pike and exhibited over Traitors' Gate within the Tower, but its lolling tongue kept its secret, and though many searched, no one is known to have found the Lieutenant's loot.

Some attempts were made, of course. In October of the same year Samuel Pepys heard of the treasure from Lord Sandwich and obtained the king's warrant to search. Not with the intention of returning the proceeds to the victims of Barstead's greed, however. Instead, it was agreed that the king would receive £3000, with £2000 each for Lord Sandwich and Pepys. So Pepys, having left his sword with the yeoman warder at the gate, met his assistants Evett and Wade, who claimed to know the hiding place. Hours of laborious digging followed, in various cellars and vaults, in and around the Lieutenant's Lodgings and the adjoining Bell Tower. To save time, meals were taken on the head of a barrel amidst the piles of earth in the candle-lit gloom, but nothing was found. Two more attempts in November disillusioned Pepys and he gave up the search. So the Tower of London jealously guards two prizes of great value. Everyone knows where the Crown Jewels are, but who will find Barkstead's treasure?

The wealth amassed by that gentleman and other Lieutenants came not from their pay but, like the Constable's income, from the perquisites of the appointment. At one time the salary was only £20 a year, but the Lieutenant was entitled to a tax on all prisoners in the Tower on a percentage basis, bringing him in £2 for every £75 of the prisoner's income. This, in a state prison whose inmates were noblemen with vast estates, meant a lucrative career for the man in charge.

Another profitable sideline was the sale of furnishings. A prisoner arriving at the Tower would be allocated an empty prison room and he had to supply the necessary furniture, wall-hangings, crockery and the like from his own house or resources. Most home comforts were essential, for the stone walls were cold and bleak, and he was likely to spend many years there. The benefit to the Lieutenant lay in the regulation stipulating that all furnishings were forfeited to him when the prisoner was executed, released or, a rather remote possibility, escaped. The goods and chattels so obtained were then resold to other new arrivals, providing the officer with a continuous income.

Other perquisites included a levy of wine from passing ships – the Tower Bottles, as stated earlier, being stored in his cellars – and also a share of fish caught in the Thames. These, and other benefits, were abolished by royal decree in the sixteenth century, a fixed salary of £150 a year being paid instead. A century later, this was increased by Charles II to £2,500, but it wasn't always paid!

One benefit which did continue was the sale of warderships. As described later in this chapter, the Lieutenant had the duty to keep the Body of Yeoman Warders up to strength, receiving payment by selling vacancies. Alas, James II put an end to this in 1688. And a few years later the Lieutenants ceased to live in the Tower, though even now, during their three-year term of office, they take over the duties of the Constable or Resident Governor should it be necessary.

Majors and Governors

Just as the Lieutenant was deputy to the Constable, so he had two deputies of his own, one known as the Deputy Lieutenant, the other as the Major of the Tower. Before his execution in 1747, Lord Lovat is reported to have said to Richard White, Major of the Tower, 'I am preparing myself, Sir, for a place where hardly any Majors and very few Deputy Lieutenants go' (Younghusband, page 90). But he didn't specify which place! The two appointments gradually merged until, just over a hundred years ago, the man having command of the Tower of London had the title 'Major and Resident Governor'.

Today, the Constable is of course still involved in high-level decisions concerning the Tower, as is the Resident Governor, and the latter has the added responsibility of the day-to-day administration and control of the Tower, and is also Keeper of the Jewel House. He is therefore a member of the royal household. Always an Army officer of the rank of general, he lives in the Queen's House and his term of office is five years. Together with his deputy governors and yeoman warders, he is host to visiting royalty and foreign dignitaries, presidents, princes and the millions of tourists who throng the Tower each year.

Recruiting the Warders, Then and Now

There is little doubt that the post of yeoman warder was much sought after. A house within the walls was provided, although this sometimes entailed having a prisoner as a paying guest, and a more or less regular wage was paid, together with a uniform and weapons.

As already mentioned, one of the perquisites of the Lieutenant of the Tower was the sale of vacant warderships to men of his choice. Human nature being as frail then as it is today, some unscrupulous Lieutenants realised that their income would be increased by employing old and infirm men who would rapidly need replacing! The effect of this must have turned the Warders' Hall into something resembling an old folk's home, and it would seem that younger applicants protested strongly, for on 22 November 1623, the king's secretary wrote to the Lieutenant: 'The King requires you instantly to admit John Oxenton, who has applied for the next wardership, a place now being vacant, or to state the grounds upon which he has been refused, both on this and a previous vacancy.' Such pressure from high places brought quick results. On 8 December a further letter from the secretary signified the king's pleasure at John Oxenton being sworn in and admitted to a warder's place.

Obviously though, such malpractices by the Lieutenant could not be tolerated, and by royal decree on 10 July 1688, the selling of warderships was prohibited, James II ordering that 'no officer of the Tower shall henceforth presume to sell the said office or receive any gratuity for the appointment of a yeoman

Yeoman Warder, 1785

warder, or admit any person unto that office, but such as shall be first approved of by His Majesty'.

Instead, warders purchased the post from resigning members and, in turn, sold their warderships when they left. The system obviously improved matters considerably, for in 1696, a mere eight years later, John Tedder paid the required sum to a retiring warder – and died, still a warder, in October 1758, after sixty-two years and nine months service in the Tower! Alas, by dying in harness instead of leaving and selling the vacancy, his money was not repaid to his family but went instead to the Constable.

The purchase price was fixed at 250 guineas (£262.50) which

was a vast sum in those days. This was in addition to minor sums payable to the Constable (£21), his secretary (£6.30), the rest of the warders (£5.25) and other incidentals. To retire eventually and sell one's wardership was obviously to be desired, but should a warder die before retirement, the Constable of the Tower then sold the vacancy and made a clear profit of nearly £300. The Tower Records of 1735 quote another such case: 'Thomas Curry, yeoman warder, being deceased, the Constable has signed and delivered a Warrant to Richard Laming for £262.10.0, he being recommended as warder by Colonel Williamson, Deputy Lieutenant of the Tower'. This dire possibility gave rise to the Warder's Toast, used to this very day, 'May you never die a Yeoman Warder!'

While this method produced younger men, they weren't necessarily of the calibre demanded by such responsible tasks. Indeed, the seventeenth and eighteenth centuries saw a sad deterioration in standards, with prisoners being able to escape and warders neglecting their duties, some even renting out their houses in the Tower and living elsewhere.

In 1722, Yeoman Warder William Wilkins somehow arranged with the authorities not to come to work at all, and for sixteen years he continued in his chosen profession as an innkeeper at Newington Butts, Southwark, on the other bank of the river! Perhaps in appreciation of the extra work his absence inflicted on his fellow warders, he presented them with a large and handsome bowl which is still a prized possession in the Tower. It is made of pewter and engraved with the date 1725 and the words 'God Preserve King George and the Royal Family'; the underside bears the initials 'WW' after the donor. It is believed to have been used as a punchbowl by the warders, but it now plays an important part in the 'swearing in' of a new warder.

All royal servants had to declare their allegiance to their sovereign and, of course, the warders were no exception. The oath they swear today varies very little from that used in October 1727 (see Appendix). There was, however, a version at the turn of this century which decreed that the yeoman warder being sworn in could not be arrested or detained as prisoner without the Constable's consent. He was also exempted from having to bear office as a church warden, scavenger, collector or the like. No jury service would be enforced, nor would he be chargeable with any kind of taxes or payment. Oh, to have been a Victorian yeoman warder!

The practice of holding a Swearing In Ceremony lapsed for a number of years recently until, after research by the author and with the good offices of the then Resident Governor, Major General Sir Digby Raeburn CB, DSO, MBE, the procedure was revived in the 1970s.

After the Tower has been closed to the public, the yeoman warders in Undress uniform, form a semicircle on Tower Green. The new warder stands in the centre, facing the Resident Governor and his deputies in their resplendent uniforms. The applicant holds the Bible and repeats the Warder's Oath after the Resident Governor. The Chief Yeoman Warder (the title which replaced that of Yeoman Porter) then requests permission for the Body of Yeoman Warders to adjourn to their club within the walls. All assemble therein, and glasses are charged from the Swearing In Bowl described above. In the presence of the officers, the Chief Warder makes a brief speech of welcome to the new warder. All those present then raise their glasses in the ancient and traditional toast to him: 'May you never die a Yeoman Warder!'

This is just an historic greeting, for the purchasing of warderships was discontinued in 1827 by the Constable of the Tower, the famous Duke of Wellington. He was determined to improve the calibre of his men and so decreed that 'none but deserving, gallant and meritorious discharged serjeants of the Army shall be appointed Warders of the Tower' (Tower Records). Eligibility is now limited to warrant officers and their equivalent ranks, and the Royal Air Force and Royal Marines also qualify, though not the Royal Navy. This exception may be because, historically, seamen of the Navy rarely volunteered for service with the Crown but were recruited forcibly by press-gangs, and therefore had never sworn allegiance to the sovereign.

In addition to the required rank, applicants must have served for at least twenty-two years, possess an honourable service record and be recommended for the appointment by their commanding officers. Following an interview of the applicant and his wife by the Resident Governor, and approval by the Constable, the successful candidate is placed on the waiting list. But as there are less than forty yeoman warders in the world, 'many are called, but few are chosen'! (It is of interest to note that the time served in the armed forces by the present Body of Yeoman Warders totals over one thousand years.)

In addition to joining the Body of Yeoman Warders, each new warder also attends St James's Palace, there to be sworn in as a Member of the Queen's Bodyguard of the Yeomen of the Guard Extraordinary. The details of this honour, and the name of the recipient, are entered on a handsome Certificate designed by the Queen's Scribe, Donald Jackson. The document, signed by the Constable of the Tower, is highly treasured by the holder.

Subject to good health and performance, warders may remain at the Tower until retirement at the age of sixty-five though they can retire at sixty on pension if they wish.

3 Uniform and Weapons

Oh, I would a Yeoman Warder be
With tunic aflare from neck to knee.
Partizan held so straight and steady
That it could be said I was Ruff'd and Ready!
But only in jest I'd have ye know
For across my chest in manly row
Are strung the medals I won in defence
Of truth and right and common sense.
Oh, I would a Yeoman Warder be –
Say, who is the man who would stand with me?

The earliest record of a yeoman warder uniform is of the previously mentioned adoption of the Yeomen of the Guard uniform in 1550, with the exception of the crossbelt. It is believed that this Tudor uniform was designed by the Court painter Hans Holbein. Basically, it is the same as is worn today on state occasions, but during four hundred years it is inevitable that minor changes have occurred, reflecting differing fashions and working conditions.

To wear the State Dress uniform is to feel hot, constricted, but utterly splendid! The Tudor bonnet, high crowned and broad brimmed, sits square, and is made of black velvet trimmed with ribbons of the Queen's colours. The ruff, of bleached Irish linen, keeps the chin up, holds the head almost immovable and cushions the beard wonderfully. Between parades, it (the ruff not the beard) is usually kept gently flattened in a trouser-press, for a ruff with ripples looks rough! This adornment buttons tightly at the back, its hem tucked into the collar of the coat, which is a magnificent garment reaching to the knee.

Of royal scarlet, the coat is embellished on skirt, sleeves and swordbelt with lines of gold braid on each side of strips of black velvet. Chest and back have the royal crown and heraldic Tudor rose, with the thistle and shamrock and the letters ER (Elizabeth Regina) embroidered in gold thread. Medals and decorations are, of course, worn and these add further lustre. Scarlet breeches are held tight below the knee by gold braid, and scarlet stockings and black shoes complete the attire.

Shoe bows and knee bows – rosettes made up of bows of red, white and blue ribbon – are worn on the instep and at the side of the knee. With sword in scabbard and 8ft (2.4m) partizan in white-gloved hands, the final effect is sheer pageantry and well worth the hour's toil in donning it all. The sensation is that of being a three dimensional king-sized playing card! To see the Body of Yeoman Warders on parade in full State Dress, dims all other uniforms into dull mediocrity – and rightly so.

The Chief Warder carries his wand of office, a silver replica of the White Tower on a polished wooden staff dating from 1792, instead of a partizan; and his armbadge bears, beneath a crown, four gold stripes with crossed keys, recalling his earlier title of Yeoman Porter. The Yeoman Gaoler, the senior of the two when the Tower was a thriving prison, is now deputy to the Chief Warder. His sleeve also bears a crown and four stripes but has the White Tower embroidered thereon. He carries the ceremonial axe, its blade 20in (50cm) long and 10in (25cm) wide, on a 5ft 4in (1.6m) wooden shaft with four rows of burnished brass nails down the sides. It dates from the sixteenth century and was used, when escorting a prisoner, to indicate to the watching crowds the verdict of the court. The edge of the axe pointing towards the prisoner meant the death sentence, and rarely did it point away!

A third appointment is that of Yeoman Clerk, his badge being four plain gold stripes beneath a crown, and he carries a partizan as do the warders. This weapon, a type of pike, has the insignia of the reigning monarch on its sharp pointed blade, and at the top of the wooden staff is a handsome red and gold silk tassel, 9 in (22cm) in length. Each warder is issued with and wears a sword – an elegant, beautifully balanced weapon designed to maintain order among the prisoners and, of course, to defend the Tower against any onslaught. To help the warders resist temptation, they are not carried when the Tower is open to the public!

In earlier days the uniform varied, for centuries lacking the thistle and shamrock emblems. Queen Elizabeth I added the ruff, and on 26 August 1597 'The Queen's Embroiderer was

The Yeoman Warder's uniform between 1858 and 1885. Note the Tudor bonnet worn with Undress uniform

paid £88 9s 4½d for embroidering with roses and crowns the red coats given to the ordinary yeomen of the chamber, the warders of the Tower, the yeomen of the robes and beds, and the five messengers of the chamber' (Calendar of State Papers, Domestic series). During her reign the warders had to buy their own weapons, and if armed attack threatened, they donned helmet and breastplate. In later reigns stockings were white or grey, and the rosettes were omitted. Stuart warders had plumed hats, with lace replacing ruffs, whereas in the eighteenth century a grey collar encircled the neck, and hats were flat and soft.

The coronation of George III resulted in a royal letter to the Master of the Great Wardrobe for

… forty coats of fine crimson in grain cloth, lined with blue serge and guarded with blue velvet, edged and lined with gold lace, with rose, thistle and crown, mottoes and scrowles, with our letters G R embroidered on back and breast of each coat, with silver spangles gilt, for the Warders of our Tower of London. With forty pair of like crimson cloth breeches, guarded with velvet and laced with gold lace; forty black velvet bonnets with crimson, white and blue ribands; forty pair of grey worsted rowling stockings; forty basket-hilted swords with brass hilts and silver handles, double gilt; forty partizans chased and gilt, with cowls of crimson, skye colour and white silk. Forty waistbelts and forty pair of buck gloves. Also £40 for Watchcoats for them, and a large Bible bound in rough leather for the use of our Warders at the Tower. Given under our signet at the Palace of St James's this 29th day of May 1761 in the first year of our reign.

An order on the books of 1763 required the warders 'to wear a wig with one curl when on duty'. This doubtless gave rise to an application submitted by the warders in May 1795 to the Inland Revenue, to be exempted from the hair powder duty tax, they being servants of His Majesty. Plea rejected!

The State Dress, which is tailored for the wearer, is very expensive and difficult to keep immaculate. It is now only worn when royalty visits the Tower and for special ceremonies and church parades. This arrangement was made possible because in 1858 Queen Victoria approved a blue Undress uniform. The newspapers of the day, and *Punch* magazine, lamented loud and long at this appalling tampering with tradition, but economy triumphed, and so it is the normal working dress at the Tower.

The coat is the same shape as that of the State Dress and is dark blue adorned with red ribbon. On the chest is a large royal crown in red, below which is the insignia of the reigning monarch. Long trousers are worn – dark blue with a red stripe on the outsides – and brass-buckled belt and black shoes. Black gloves and a red-lined cape may be worn in bad weather. And until 1885 the Tudor bonnet was worn with the uniform, but then a matching hat was issued. Similar in shape to the Tudor bonnet, it is dark blue with a red and blue cockade in front and a red ribbon around the base of the crown.

This Undress uniform, smart if lacking the Tudor splendour, is at least more practical for normal working purposes. The coat has no lapels, thus depriving drunks of a useful 'handhold', and being voluminous, it allows various thicknesses of shirts to be worn beneath for added warmth. Wearing the uniform in hot weather is, however, to be slowly broiled. Its dark colour, high and tight neckband and close-buttoned cuffs convert it into a mobile sauna. 'Stand in the sun and smile!' demand the tourists. Ah well, if one wants the glamour, one has to suffer! And when the public has been shepherded out, the uniform coats are taken off, turned inside out and hung on the clothes-line – to drip!

Both uniforms are worn with variations on other occasions. For state events such as the sovereign's birthday or the State opening of Parliament, Semi State Dress is worn, comprising the Tudor bonnet and State Dress coat with the Undress trousers and shoes – but no sword! For the duty of Watchman of the Tower, a long red coat is worn with the Undress hat and trousers – the same style of watchcoat as was ordered by George III in 1761, and not forgetting John of London's 'Rugg Gown' of 1321. The Chief Warder is similarly clad when locking and unlocking the gates night and morning, though he wears his Tudor bonnet.

So the warders' range of uniforms is both expensive and extensive. Every item must be maintained to the highest standard in order to enhance the dignity of the Tower and to impress the public, as tourists' photograph albums all over the world will testify.

4 Guarding the Prisoners

Will ye give me your mantle, kind sir?
'Tis my right, to claim such a token
In spite of your plight.
I can sell it for kindling
For meat or for bread,
And remember – remember
'Ere they sever your head
Ye will care much the less
For things such as that –
  'Will I now,' said Sir Thomas –
  And gave him his hat!

Not only did the warders keep the enemies of the king out of the Tower by guarding the gates, they also kept them in, as prisoners. From Bishop Flambard in 1100 to Rudolf Hess in 1941, captive kings and queens, nobles and Jesuits, traitors and plotters were incarcerated in the Tower, many suffering eventual death beneath the axe, or by fire or the rope.

Despite high walls and deep moat, a few achieved the seemingly impossible and got away; the warders responsible were of course severely punished. When Lord Nithsdale escaped in 1716 dressed as a woman, five warders lost their secure jobs, despite their long service: Cook and Mason, who had been warders for twenty-five years, Baber with nineteen years' service, Bird with eleven and Davidge with ten. In 1597 Warder Bonner, yielding to bribery and blackmail, assisted the Jesuit priest John Gerard to escape and then had to flee himself, outlawed for life; his wife was later caught and punished. These warders were let off lightly, however, compared with William Tasborough and John Gillet. They should have been guarding John Tudor, a prisoner who, in May 1654, fled to safety.

Tasborough and Gillet not only lost their jobs but, ironically, were themselves gaoled in the Tower.

Another warder to be dismissed and fortunate not to receive more severe penalties, was Robert Brownlow. He was guarding Donough MacCarthy, 4th Earl of Clancarty, who was imprisoned in 1690 for supporting the claims of James II. In March 1695 the earl applied to leave the Tower in order to visit a nearby bagnio, this being described variously as a bath-house or a brothel! Upon surety of £400, plus a further £100 from each of four friends, and also on condition that Warder Brownlow escorted him, permission was granted. No record exists as to why the warder neglected his duty, but the earl managed to escape, eventually reaching the Continent. Robert Brownlow, returning minus prisoner, was immediately dismissed. The earl was later recaptured and confined in Newgate Gaol for many years.

Assisting the prisoners in any way brought retribution, as when, on 25 February 1723, 'Warder Cousins was discharged with disgrace on Suspition of roguery, in that he did supply a prisoner with paper, Pens and ink in proportion, also a new Pensill, to send messages out of the Tower' (Fox, page 38). Two of the Lieutenant's servants were also punished for helping a female prisoner escape during the reign of Henry VIII, one being dismissed, the other racked and hanged.

It should not be forgotten that in addition to the famous women held in the Tower, many lesser-known ones suffered its bleak hospitality. One such was Lady Badlesmere who, with her husband, owned that well-fortified residence, Leeds Castle in Kent. In 1322 Queen Isabella, en route from Canterbury to London, decided to break her arduous journey and stay the night at the nearest castle. So, as was the custom, she sent her messengers on ahead to notify the Badlesmeres of her imminent arrival.

Lady Badlesmere, aware of her absent husband's opposition to King Edward II, not only raised the drawbridge but had the queen's representatives killed. Retribution followed fast. Edward personally led the onslaught, and despite moat, drawbridge and portcullis, Leeds Castle was overwhelmed. The officer in charge and his subordinates were hanged, and Lady Badlesmere was committed to the Tower, her ultimate fate being unknown.

In 1441, the Duchess of Gloucester and a Mrs Jourdayn were

accused of sorcery and witchcraft against the king and imprisoned in the Tower. The duchess was later released, but Jourdayn was burnt to death at Smithfield. And another who died in the same horrific way was Anne Askew, in 1545. She had been accused of heresy and of conspiring with Queen Katherine Parr against Henry VIII. In order to obtain a complete confession, she was cruelly racked in the vaults of the White Tower, until she fainted with the agony. In the following year the fires of Smithfield claimed another victim.

The early 1600s must have been a hectic time for the warders. There was the coronation of James I, followed by the long imprisonment of Raleigh in the Bloody Tower. Guy Fawkes and his fellow conspirators were caught, interrogated and executed, and then there was a high-level enquiry into the escape of the Duke of Somerset and his wife, Arabella Stuart, who died insane in the Queen's House some years later.

But the most bizarre affair was the systematic poisoning of a prisoner, Sir Thomas Overbury, by his two enemies Robert Carr and Lady Francis Howard, in 1613. Lady Francis had been supplied with corrosive poisons by Mrs Anne Turner, a woman of evil repute at Court. Overbury died a hideous death, although the Tower Coroner's jury of six yeoman warders and six prisoners brought in a verdict of 'death from natural causes'! Justice triumphed, however, and all the plotters were arrested. Lady Francis and Robert Carr were imprisoned, she in the very room in which her victim had suffered so excruciatingly.

Mrs Turner wore a new hat and a yellow ruff at her trial, a fashion she had introduced by inventing the yellow starch required. She was found guilty and condemned to death. The judge further ordered that when hanged she was to wear the yellow ruff she had brought into vogue. She was executed on 9 November 1615, before a vast crowd at Tyburn. As ordered, she wore a large yellow ruff, and in heavy jest the public hangman also wore one, made of bright yellow paper. Yellow starched ruffs immediately went out of fashion.

Another topic of interest that caused much discussion in the Warder's Hall in the Byward Tower later that century concerned a man from the American colonies. Edward Grove from Hampton, New England, had been caught on 6 June 1684, conspiring against the king. Brought before Edward Cranfield, Lieutenant Governor of New Hampshire, he was charged with 'levying war against Charles II' (Bayley, page 595). Found

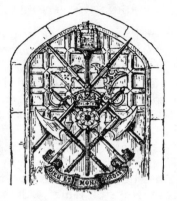

Yeoman Warders' Trophy of Arms

guilty, he was shipped to England and there confined in the Tower 'during His Majesty's Pleasure'.

A much more colourful character from our mutinous colonies was Henry Laurens, the wealthy Vice-President of South Carolina. He considered that since France and Spain were actively supporting his countrymen in their fight for independence against England, perhaps Holland could be persuaded to do the same – for certain financial inducements, of course.

In August 1780 he set sail but didn't get very far, for after a brief skirmish off the coast of Newfoundland, his ship was captured. His baggage was searched, and the incriminating papers involving Holland were found. There was only one place for him, and on 6 October 1780, as the yeoman warders on duty whistled 'Yankee Doodle' in welcome, he was escorted into the Tower of London. There he was confined for a year, living with and being guarded by a warder in a house on Tower Green. He was well treated, friends being allowed to visit him, but he later wrote an account complaining bitterly about the conditions and the warders.

Towards the end of 1781 he was released on bail, and in the following year was exchanged for Lord Cornwallis after the latter's defeat at Yorktown. In that way the Tower relinquished one man but gained another, for Lord Cornwallis at that time was also Constable of the Tower. Henry Laurens returned to America and frequently 'dined out' on his experiences, adopting the nickname 'Tower' Laurens. He deserved his brief moment of fame, for the discovery of his papers did after all lead to war with Holland – and Laurens left the Tower with his head intact!

A warder's life, however, wasn't all whistling popular songs and parading at coronations. The job had its risks, as for instance in April 1671, when the notorious Colonel Blood fired his pistol at a warder in a vain attempt to escape with the Crown Jewels, the same precious items which police and warders so daringly rescued during a disastrous fire in the Tower 170 years later.

Violent prisoners, too, were always a hazard, one such causing the brutal murder of a warder. Peter Burchet, a fanatic who believed that no sin was committed when killing anyone who disagreed with his particular religious beliefs, had been accused of stabbing Sir John Hawkins with a dagger. On the day in question, 10 November 1573, Burchet was in his prison room in the Beauchamp Tower, under the guard of two warders. One of them having left the room, Burchet suddenly picked up a length of wood from the open fire and attacked the other warder, Hugh Longworth, who had been reading a Bible in the window recess. Repeated blows felled the warder, Burchet 'leaving him not till he had stryken him starke dead' (Bayley, page 159).

Justice was swift and merciless. The following day the murderer was tried at Westminster and condemned, the penalty being exacted twenty-four hours later. For striking a blow within a royal palace – severing of the right hand at the wrist; for the act of murder – death by hanging.

Generally though, relationships between prisoners and their guardians were good. Understandably so, as many high ranking prisoners were housed in their warders' residences within the Tower and paid their 'hosts' for food and service. The rate in the mid-eighteenth century was £10 per annum for lodging and 1s (5p) a day for the warder. One such prisoner was William, Lord Byron, great uncle of the poet, who was accused of treason in 1765. He lived at no. 4 Tower Green, in the house of Yeoman Warder George Jervis, though bars had to be fitted over the windows of his room.

The warders had to ensure that no one approached their prisoners without the Lieutenant's permission, and that no communication with outside accomplices took place. Not only had the prisoners' barber to be a yeoman warder, but in 1722 a regulation declared that where a warder had no wife or relative to do the shopping for household and prisoner, 'a reliable maid should deputise and all maids to go at 9am accompanied by one warder to prevent passing of messages to others' (Fox, page 30). Such a procession must have been quite a sight in the local market!

This boarding house arrangement suited the warders, whose wages were never lavish. In Elizabeth I's time they received 6d (2½p) per day; by 1747 this had only doubled, and two warders, Misenigoe and Jollif, were indicted in the records as trouble-making ringleaders agitating for a pay rise. Sometimes protests were justified, for on 17 May 1678 the warders petitioned King Charles II because they had received no pay for three years: 'they had paid for their own food and clothing and if they did not get their pay they were like to be ruined' (Preston, page 145). The result, familiar in these days, was that they got their pay, but their numbers were reduced by natural wastage, from forty to twenty-four!

Some three centuries later, in 1951, more pay was requested when the Tower was opened to the public on Sunday after-noons. Mindful of their military rather than militant back-ground, the warders did not specify any particular amount. 'We leave it to you,' they told the Resident Governor. They got their rise, to £5 16s 6d (£5.82½) a week.

Not only did the prisoners pay for their lodgings, but they also gave presents at Christmas. Lords Nithsdale and Derwent-water, and the Earls of Powys and Lansdowne each gave one guinea (£1.05), while even the Master of the Royal Mint, Sir Isaac Newton, contributed £1. The warders further increased their income by requesting tips from those entering the Tower, until forbidden by an order of 25 September 1724, which only allowed them 'to take mony of those who are inclin'd to give it to them but to stop or force no man to it' (Fox, page 30). The Yeoman Porter also had a traditional perquisite: he was allowed to claim the upper garment of all condemned prisoners as they were brought into the Tower. This macabre custom was en-livened in 1534 upon the arrival of Sir Thomas More at Traitors' Gate. When asked for his upper garment, he proffered his hat!

Escorting prisoners to and from Westminster Hall for trial must have provided the warders with a day out in town too, and the practice grew until, in 1715, the Lord Chancellor discovered that seven Jacobite lords and their twelve warders were adjourn-ing between court sessions to the Fountain Tavern in the Strand, there to eat roast beef (what else?), drink their port and fill their snuff boxes, to the immense interest of the watching crowd.

Westminster immediately took over the catering.

Of course, in many cases the warders were with their charges right up to the very end, having become friends with them as the months, even years, passed by. The night before Simon, Lord Lovat, was beheaded, he and his warder rehearsed the execution, using a bed pillow as the block to make sure that the old man's neck would not be too thick for the block's groove. And it was taken for granted that warders would sometimes assist their prisoners to mount the steps of the public scaffold on Tower Hill, and support them while the final prayers were said.

At the more historic executions within the walls, yeoman warders encircled the scaffold when the royal queens and others met their tragic deaths, and it is believed that it was a warder who obtained the old arrow chest in which Anne Boleyn's remains were placed for burial.

The warders' role of guarding the prisoners ended in the last century. The enemy spies executed by firing squad within the Tower during both world wars were the responsibility of army personnel, the latter also mounting guard over Rudolf Hess, Deputy Fuhrer of Germany, the U-boat crews and other German prisoners-of-war held there during World War II. However, the primary task of the warders, established over nine centuries ago, is still 'to keep watch and ward, to announce all State arrivals at the gates of the Fortress, and to detain strangers till their business be made known to the governor and orders are received for their admittance' (Tower Records). Or, as more succinctly expressed in 1730: 'No beggars or shabby rascals to be admitted through the gates, and fellows like such must tell the warders the persons names that they would speak with, before they have entrance' (Younghusband, page 101).

And so, when the post-war world and its tourists 'discovered' the Tower of London, the yeoman warders successfully revised their historic roles, becoming guards and guides to the visiting millions.

5 Present Duties

'Tis a tale I recount of sorrow and strife.
Of kingly desires and choices of wife.
Merriment surely when spirits were high,
And the telling of beads as the axe drew nigh.
Mirth I must show them in case they grow feared,
And smiles I shall exercise under my beard –
For these folks who come by to listen agape
To the Warder's fine stories of trial and escape.

Members of the public were allowed to enter the Tower as early as 1671. Colonel Blood was one of them, and his attempt to steal the Crown Jewels has made the yeoman warders wary ever since. The actual totals of visitors, however, were insignificant until improved roads and the coming of the railways encouraged the Victorians to visit their national monuments. Even then, working life in the Tower must have been very leisurely, with only about 100,000 people paying to visit the Armouries each year in the mid-1800s. Nowadays, that number pours into the Tower in a summer fortnight.

At the turn of this century, visitors waited outside until twenty-five had gathered and were then escorted by a warder to the Armouries, the Jewel House and out again. However, the sheer increase in numbers to well over 2 million a year in the 1970s and 80s called for a considerable change in organisation, and yeoman warders are now stationed at strategic places around the grounds, every warder being allocated a different post each day – twenty years in the Bloody Tower is even more than Raleigh got! The duty roster is known as the Daily Wait, from the Old French 'waite' meaning a guard or sentry, and this governs a warder's working life. For most of the year the Tower is open to the public seven days a week, so the warders look forward to their weekly day off, to changing into 'civvies' and merging with the crowds in blissful anonymity!

Some duty posts include the collection of admission tickets, which is not as menial as one might think, for this is the modern equivalent of the warder's age-old duty to check all strangers entering the Tower. Any knives or other weapons are taken from the owner, to be collected on exit. To anyone who objects, it is pointed out that a noted traveller, Paul Hentzner, visited the Tower in 1597 and complained, 'Upon entering the Tower we were obliged to quit our swords at the gate and deliver them to the guard' (Sutherland Gower, page 58). So what's new?

Being on duty anywhere in the grounds can only be described as an exhausting ego trip. Cameras, still and movie, are constantly in action, and a surreptitious scratch is out of the question. Admirers flock round, pleading in every language under the sun for photographs and for smiles, until one's teeth go dry. The sensation is somewhere between being royalty and Father Christmas for over eight hours a day, and yet the job of yeoman warder is not that of photographic model.

At the turn of this century, three police inspectors and twenty constables were on duty at the Tower. Now, the warders are sworn in instead, with full powers of arrest. The Tower has always been a target for terrorists, pickpockets, vandals and common hooligans, and it is the prime duty of the warders to protect the public from these varlets. As a sideline they also comfort lost children, obtain medical attention for the ailing, and try to be patient with those who think that the admission fee gives them squatters' rights after closing time. Wrong doers and queue jumpers are reprimanded, gently or otherwise, and not so bright questions are answered – 'No, madam, the Crown Jewels are not real, just well-sucked wine gums' and 'That is Tower Bridge, and Anne Boleyn was never imprisoned in it'. Many questions are of course intelligent and thought provoking. 'Are those really the Jewels we see, or are they reflections projected there by laser beams from down below, like holograms?' No comment!

All the harassment though is compensated for by the grateful look in dad's eyes as one holds his kids' hands for a treasured photograph, or by the tearful relief of a mother on being reunited with her lost child. So at the end of an exhausting day, a lot of people have been given a happy memory – and that's what the job is all about.

A May Day Parade in the Tower of London

Eighty years ago, visitors requiring a guided tour had to get special permission from the Resident Governor for the services of a yeoman warder. Nowadays, these tours are routinely provided throughout the day, weather permitting, although in the Daily Wait they are still called 'specials'. And on joining the Body of Yeoman Warders, the greatest hurdle is that of learning the history necessary to do specials. Colleagues coach while perambulating the moat, books are mumbled over, nightmares endured.

Just to know the history is not enough. The voice must penetrate the roar of hovering helicopters, the nearby road drill and the cacophony of London's traffic, for to use a loud-hailer would ruin the Tudor image! The accent must be understandable by Americans, Australians, self-taught Finns, and those two gentlemen at the back who are obviously waiting for the Urdu or perhaps the Swahili translation. The timing along the route is equally critical. To linger too long at one point causes following tour parties to pile up like badly shunted railway wagons. To accelerate is even worse, striking alarm and consternation in the yeoman warder ahead as his crowd suddenly doubles in size and he finds that he's half a duet.

When the new warder thinks he is ready, he undergoes an ordeal which is generally accepted as being the worst day in a warder's life. He has to prove his competency to the Resident Governor and the Chief Warder by taking them on a personal tour. This takes place before the tourists are admitted, but is still public enough to unnerve the strongest. If successful, the warder can then face the public with confidence, swaying them with his rhetoric, dazzling them with his knowledge, overwhelming them with his modesty.

Once a month or so, a warder undertakes the duty of Watchman, having the responsibility for the Tower of London from the end of one working day to the beginning of the next. The curfew bell, dated 1651, has to be rung at dusk, a practice going back to when London houses were wooden-walled and huddled close together in narrow streets. The risk of fire was great, and so the curfew warned inhabitants to 'couvre feu' – cover fires to extinguish them before going to bed. The Tower curfew urged prisoners' servants and friends to leave the castle before nightfall, or woe betide them. The Watchman, wearing his long red coat, also takes part in the Ceremony of the Keys, which is described in full in the chapter dealing with Tower ceremonies.

Their regular duties bring the yeoman warders into contact not only with the general public, but also with visiting heads of state, foreign dignitaries, ambassadors and politicians. Such meetings provide moments of interest, world leaders reacting to the fascination of the Tower in the same way as the ordinary tourists. I had the pleasure of conducting the then American President's son Chip Carter and his wife Caron around the grounds in 1977, and on another occasion I was on duty at the main gate when the son of Kenya's leader, Jomo Kenyatta, paid an official visit. Halting his limousine for identification purposes, I revived memories of my service in Africa and greeted him in Swahili, much to his astonishment. It must have been the last thing he could have expected to hear at the entrance to an ancient castle!

Not only do visitors come from all over the world, but from outside it too. In the early 1960s Yuri Gagarin, the first man in space, attracted large crowds when he came to the Tower. And in March 1981, guests within my house in the Tower included Dr David Scott and his charming wife. David Scott has been launched into space on three occasions, in Gemini 8, Apollo 9 and Apollo 15, and he is one of the very few astronauts to have walked on the moon.

In the evening as we strolled around the grounds, the moon was low over the White Tower, so I took the opportunity to point out the link between the planet and the building. Three centuries ago Charles II decreed that the heavens should be studied from the round turret of the White Tower, and in consequence the Astronomer Royal contributed much to the early records on which all subsequent research was based. So perhaps without the Tower of London, there would have been no moonwalk! David Scott was duly impressed, especially on learning that the astronomer was Sir John Flamstead, for that name is given to a large crater on the moon!

Down to earth celebrities are also never far away: beauty queens, fashion models, film stars and similar publicity seekers who find the yeoman warders ideal companions – photographically. The media is there too, with international camera crews needing historic settings and newspapers avid for stories of ravens or crowns, for the Tower is news all over the world.

Of course, the warders' duties aren't all restricted to the Tower. At countless coronations they have played their part in the pageantry at Westminster Abbey. In 1937, when George VI was crowned, the Chief Warder and twenty yeoman warders were on duty in the abbey's annexe, while Yeoman Gaoler John Fraser and six colleagues guarded the regalia in the Jerusalem Chamber within. And on a sadder note, twenty-four warders attended the king's Lying in State after his death in February 1952, taking post in the nave, choir and on the chancel steps of the abbey. Similarly, on the death of Queen Mary in 1953, twelve warders were on duty in St Paul's Cathedral.

The same year also saw the coronation of our present Queen, with fourteen yeoman warders on Jewel Guard in the abbey, their .38 revolvers contrasting strangely with their Tudor-style uniforms. Outside, twenty-one of their colleagues in State Dress guarded the entrance and annexe to Westminster Abbey, just as earlier royal guards had done on Christmas Day 1066, when William the Conqueror was crowned King of England.

Since World War II, members of the royal family have made innumerable appearances at functions in famous London buildings – the Guildhall, the Royal Festival Hall, the Opera House, Mansion House and others – and have been attended by yeoman warders in State Dress. I personally had the honour to be among those selected to attend at Buckingham Palace in June 1982 for the Inspection of the Queen's Bodyguard of the Yeomen of the Guard by Her Majesty the Queen, an experience of a lifetime.

So from guarding one's sovereign to holding a lost child, from apprehending a pickpocket to guiding a tour, the duties are complex and varied – but never dull!

6 The Ceremonies

Roses and lilies beribboned and bound
Borne to the Wakefield and laid on the ground.
Two houses of learning – a chaplain – a prayer
Paying due to a monarch who lay dying there.
* So practise his teaching if thou hast the will*
* For Eton and Cambridge remember him still.*

The Tower of London, with its Norman and Tudor buildings predominating, provides a perfect setting for the many ancient ceremonies performed within its walls. Some have fallen by the historic wayside, such as the great coronation processions to Westminster which started from the Tower. Or the Ceremony of the Order of the Bath, whereby the chosen knights kept vigil in St John's Chapel within the White Tower and meditated before the High Altar, around which their helmets and armour were hung.

The Chapel Royal of St John the Baptist also witnessed the wedding ceremony of Prince Arthur to Catherine of Aragon in 1501, an event accompanied by feasts and tournaments; and some fifty years later, Queen Mary plighted her troth there to Philip of Spain.

Sufficient ceremonies survive, however, to allow the Tower to be a living history book, as it continues to portray the pageantry of a bygone age.

The Ceremony of the Keys

This ceremony, the routine of securing the Tower's gates, has taken place nightly for over six hundred years. After all, private houses have their doors locked at night, and a royal palace is no exception. The task is carried out by the Chief Yeoman Warder, who had the earlier title of Yeoman Porter, or gateman. He is assisted by the yeoman warder on watch duty, and the gates are locked by ten o'clock every night, although the time has varied slightly over the centuries.

In the Middle Ages, and even now, London could be a violent and dangerous place, and the Chief Warder would no more consider going to the outer gates by himself than flying to the moon. And so an Escort to the Keys is provided – four soldiers of the Tower guard, who wait beneath the Bloody Tower archway. At seven minutes to ten precisely the Chief Warder, clad in red coat and Tudor bonnet and carrying the Tower Keys and an old candle lamp, joins his escort. Together, with one soldier carrying the lamp, they reach the outer gate. There the soldiers turn to face inward, ensuring that no one can creep up behind the Chief Warder and stab him in the back. They also present arms, for the Keys are, of course, the Queen's Keys.

Accompanied by the soldier bearing the lamp, to illuminate the lock, the Chief Warder secures the gates, shaking the bars as John of London was paid to do in 1321. The Keys party then retreats to the Middle Tower portal where, with the help of the Watchman, and again saluted by the escort, the huge doors are swung to and locked. This procedure is repeated at the Byward Tower, the innermost entrance, and then the Keys party proceeds to where a lone sentry stands guard before the Bloody Tower archway.

As they approach along the shadowed roadway, the sentry challenges, halting the Keys party. 'Who comes there?' he shouts, bayonet threatening. 'The Keys!' replies the Chief Warder. 'Whose Keys?' demands the sentry, and the response echoes along the high surrounding stone walls: 'Queen Elizabeth's Keys!'. Almost the same reply has been given at this spot for nearly seven hundred years, Queen Victoria's Keys, King Charles's, King James's, King Henry's Keys resounding through the Tower's passages and vaults. Thus satisfied, the sentry salutes. 'Pass, Queen Elizabeth's Keys, and all's well!'

The Chief Warder and his escort wheel beneath the archway and advance to where, drawn up on the steps leading to Tower Green, are the soldiers currently on Tower guard duty, their officer in front of them. Near the foot of the steps the Keys party halts. The Officer of the Guard, his sword flashing in the lamplight, orders his men to salute. The Chief Warder takes two paces forward, doffs his Tudor bonnet and shouts 'God Preserve Queen Elizabeth!', whereupon all those present reply

'Amen!'. And as the Chief Warder takes the Keys to safe custody in the Queen's House on Tower Green, a lone trumpeter sounds the 'Last Post', the call that was played all round the world when the British Empire flourished, the call to remind all servicemen of their fallen comrades. Amid the towers and turrets of this ancient fortress, a call to stir the emotions of the most hardened of natures.

As the first note sounds, the old clock on the Waterloo Block strikes ten o'clock, for now the 'silent hours' commence in the Tower, when only the Watchman and ever alert sentries are on duty. No vehicles move, for the great doors stay locked until morning, but residents can use the previously mentioned posterns, or wicket gates, which are set in the great doors. These are locked at midnight by the Watchman, after which time no one is allowed out. Should a medical emergency occur, a doctor lives within the grounds. If it's too late for his services, the chaplain lives next door! Residents already out of the Tower can enter up to 3am. If later than that, they must doze as best they can on Tower Hill until the great doors open again in the morning. Those doors, incidentally, have no keyholes on the outside, stolen keys thereby being useless. Each night a password is in force and this is changed daily. It is authorised by the Queen and is known in advance to only a few.

The description of the procedure in the reign of George II (Francis, page 215) illustrates how little this ceremony has changed during the last two or more centuries:

The Keys are lodged in the Warders Hall till the time of locking at ten of night. After locking all gates, the yeoman porter and guard proceed to the main guard, who are all under arms with the officers on duty at their head. The usual challenge from the main guard to the yeoman porter is 'Who comes there?' His answer is 'The Keys'. The challenger says 'Pass, Keys', upon which the officer orders the guard to rest their firelocks [salute]; the yeoman porter then says 'God save King George'. 'Amen' is loudly answered by all the guard. From the main guard the yeoman porter proceeds to the Governor's, where the Keys are left; after which no person can go out or come in upon any pretence whatsoever till next morning, without the watchword for the night which is kept so secret that none but the proper officers and the sergeant upon guard ever come to the knowledge of it; for it is the same on the same night in every fortified place throughout the King's Dominions. When that is given by any stranger to the sentinel at the outer gate he communicates it to his sergeant, who passes it to the next on duty, and so on till it comes to the Governor or commanding officer, by whom the Keys are delivered to the yeoman porter, who, attended as before, the main guard being put under arms, brings the Keys to the outer gate where the stranger is admitted and conducted to the Governor. Having made known his business, he is conducted to the outer gate, dismissed, the gate shut, and the Keys redelivered with all the formality as at first.

The ceremony hasn't always gone smoothly. A complication arose on 22 January 1901 when, at 7pm, Queen Victoria died. The new sovereign, Albert Edward, had not decided what name he should bear as king, and so that night at the Tower the Chief Warder raised his Tudor bonnet and proclaimed 'God preserve – the King!'. The next day came the announcement declaring 'King Edward' to be the chosen name. But what of the ceremony in Cromwell's time, when there was no sovereign? It can only be assumed that they were 'The Commonwealth's Keys'.

During World War II, with air raids in progress, steel helmets replaced Tudor bonnets. On 29 December 1940 the guardroom by the Bloody Tower was ablaze from incendiary bombs, while on 16 April 1941 the Chief Warder, the Watchman and the escort were blown off their feet by a near miss from a high-explosive bomb. Shaken but unhurt, they formed up again and of course completed the ceremony.

No ceremony accompanies the morning unlocking of the gates, for the castle is awake and so cannot be caught napping!

Changing of the Guard

Yet another frequent ceremony, held every morning in summer and alternate mornings in winter, is the Changing of the Guard. The Tower nowadays has no permanent garrison, regiments taking it in turn to provide the Tower Guard and remaining on duty for twenty-four or forty-eight hours. All Army regiments, as well as the Royal Air Force Regiment are eligible, and they regard the duty as an honour. While at the Tower, they are subordinate to the yeoman warders, who hold the equivalent rank of regimental sergeant major and are addressed accordingly.

At the end of their tour of duty, the 'Old Guard' marches on to Tower Green near the execution site. The 'New Guard' parades on the opposite side and the two officers conclude the official hand-over. As the bugles salute, the Old Guard marches off, to be transported to its home barracks, while the New Guard occupies the Waterloo Block, having assumed responsibility for the Tower's safety from attack.

It is a colourful spectacle, especially in summer when the soldiers wear their red tunics and imposing black bearskins. Interestingly enough, Dutch soldiers were on guard in the Tower in the reign of William of Orange.

Gun Salutes

On occasions such as the State Opening of Parliament, the Queen's Birthday and visits to London by foreign royalty, a gun salute is fired from the Tower Wharf, usually at about midday. The yeoman warders, wearing Semi State Dress, ie scarlet and gold coat, dark blue trousers and Tudor bonnet, are of course on duty. They cordon off the area and marshal the crowds as the Honourable Artillery Company arrive with their four 25-pounder field guns. At the appointed time, the deafening roar

28 February 1846: firing the Tower Guns to celebrate the victories in India

sends the gulls and pigeons winging high into the sky, and tourists and children cover their ears and shriek!

For the Queen's Birthday sixty-two rounds are fired, this being the number of guns which once lined the Wharf and battlements. Gun salutes fired from the Tower saluted famous victories and royal births: 'You are immediately to fire the Guns on the Wharf Battery, on the occasion of the surrender of the Dutch Fleet to the British forces at the Cape of Good Hope, 3 November 1796' and 'You will this day at One o'clock fire the Wharf guns on the occasion of the Safe delivery of a Princess to the Princess of Wales, 7 January 1796' (Source unknown).

In bygone days such events were accompanied by official festivities, as reported in the Deputy Lieutenant's diary for 1 March 1728 (Fox, page 52).

This being Queen Caroline's birth day We fired our guns round the ramparts; the Warders were all ordered to be at my doore, as I was commanding officer, where we drank the Kings, the Queens, Prince Frederick and the rest of the Royall Familys health; Prosperity to the Tower of London, the Constable, his officers and Warders, in all 5 healths. This we did in good Port wine while our guns were firing, and afterwards I ordered the Warders to form a circkle about the Officers and after the Yeoman Porter's crying with a loud voice 'God preserve King George, Queen Caroline and the Rest of the Royal Family!' I dismiss'd them to finish the Joy of the Day with the remaining part of 24 bottles of wine, which the King allows on the birth days of him selfe and Royal Consort, to his Warders and Gunners, viz: 21 to the 40 Warders and 3 to the Gunners. At night we had a bonfire on Tower Hill and a barill of beer was given to ye Serjeant and 12 men who were sent to guard it.

Not much 'Joy of the Day' occurred on 4 June 1763, however, when the crowds on Tower Hill were celebrating the king's birthday with bonfires, drinking and merry-making. People had been assembling since early in the morning, streaming in with their children from the outlying villages, and by midday many hundreds were present. In high spirits their cheers rang out with every salvo of the Tower's guns, and the roistering continued throughout the afternoon, for a firework display had been promised as soon as it was dusk.

As the afternoon wore on, a vast multitude built up, and the press of bodies was so great that the railings enclosing the Tower Hill well finally gave way, precipitating helpless spectators into its waters 30ft (9m) below. Six people were killed and fifteen injured, many severely. Nor was that all. In the confusion, a sailor who had had his pocket picked seized the thief and threw him into the moat. Fireworks forgotten, fighting broke out between other sailors and a crowd of drunken dockers, and in the riot that followed, houses were broken into, windows broken and wagons overturned.

Another jubilant event with an unhappy ending was the coronation of Anne Boleyn, on 31 May 1533, the procession to Westminster Abbey starting from the Tower. Anne had arrived from Greenwich Palace two days earlier, sailing up the River Thames with the afternoon tide, to be greeted by scores of musicians in gaily bedecked barges, boats filled with costumed performers and thousands of excited spectators on the shore. Beneath a canopy of gold and surrounded by his bodyguard, Henry VIII awaited her, and as she stepped on to Tower Wharf there was heard 'such a pele of gonnes as hathe not byn heard lyke a great while before' (Sutherland Gower, page 131).

Alas, a mere three years later, a single cannon-shot fired from the roof of the White Tower informed Henry that the axe had descended on 'her lytel neck', and he was free to marry again.

Church Parades

Three times a year, at Christmas, Easter and Whitsun, a church parade is held, the yeoman warders wearing their State Dress with swords and partizans. Resplendent in their pageantry, they line up outside the Queen's House to be inspected by the Resident Governor in his general's uniform. The chapel bell rings – the bell engraved 'John Hodgson made me 1659 IB' and believed to have been recast from the original bell which hung there. And so the sound heard today is that which tolled sonorously as the doomed queens were executed, their remains to be interred beneath the altar.

After the inspection, the Resident Governor leads the dignified column into the Chapel Royal of St Peter ad Vincula for the service, together with members of the public. This has been the custom for many years: Samuel Pepys in his diary for 1661 says, 'After dinner to chapel in the Tower with the Lieutenant, and the warders and gentlemen porter going before us'. And more recently, General and Mrs Dwight D. Eisenhower worshipped with the warders in 1962. Members of the present royal family have, of course, attended church service there on several occasions.

Although the partizans are left in the crypt, swords are retained and complicate the necessary kneeling! The chapel royal is thus one of the few churches where armed men worship, harking back to when the warders escorted royal and other prisoners into church. Swords were retained in case a sudden rescue attempt be made while all were praying.

In those early days, incidentally, congregations did not sit, but stood or knelt to worship. There were no pews or chairs in churches, only a narrow bench which ran round the sides for the benefit of the old or infirm, hence the saying 'The weakest go to the wall'.

Beating the Bounds

Henry VIII, apprehensive of revolt in the City of London, decreed that houses bordering the moat of the Tower must be demolished so that attackers could not use them as cover. This measure would give his guns, mounted on towers and walls, a clear field of fire. So the bounds or boundaries of the Tower were, in the sixteenth century, a cannon-shot distance away.

But the tradition of Beating the Bounds goes beyond that, for even the Anglo-Saxons staked out the extent of their encampments. In the Middle Ages, boys of the village would be 'whacked' at each stone, so making an impression on their minds as well! Nowadays it is the actual boundary stones which are struck, and at the Tower this ceremony is enacted every third year on Ascension Day, although in 1381 Richard II decreed that 'The said Constable shall upon every Ascension Daie goe in procession worshipfully about the Tower, having with him his Lieutenant and all the freemen and inhabitants within the Tower in their best arraye'. And everyone is in his 'best arraye', with the yeoman warders in full State Dress.

The procession, led by the Chief Warder, comprises the warders in twos, the Chaplain and the children of the Tower carrying long willow wands. Then follows the Resident Governor and his officers, and the families of the warders and other

Beating the Bounds, pre-1939

residents. In 1957 Adlai Stevenson, the United States presidential candidate, joined the line and enjoyed himself immensely! The traffic in the City of London, rarely less than nose to tail, is halted to allow access to the boundary stones, and the sheer disbelief on the faces of the drivers is as much a sight as the procession! The column wends its way, stopping at the thirty or so stones, each marked with the broad arrow. At each stone the Chaplain warns 'Cursed is he who removeth his neighbour's landmark' and the Chief Warder shouts 'Whack it, boys, whack it' as the willow wands belabour the inoffensive boundary marks.

Regrettably not only the stones were whacked in 1698, when the authorities of the nearby All Hallows Church challenged some of the Tower's boundaries. To quote the church records, 'some of the said warders broake their partizans or halberts in striking the said Churchwardens and those that were with them, but they had nothing in their hands to make any defence'. I hasten to add that we are all friends now!

The procession gradually circles round the Tower, growing longer as tourists, children and the downright curious join it, until after about an hour's perambulation it re-enters the grounds by an opposite gate. And on Tower Green, after a short prayer and a hymn, the procession disperses, the boundaries safely checked for another three years.

At one time the ceremony finished rather more sumptuously. Ascension Day 1723 ended with

> ... ye tables being spread, we regaled ourselves with an entertainment of three cold hams, bread and butter, radishes etc. and several bottles of wine, where His Majesty, ye Prince and Princess and ye rest of ye Royal Family's health were drank. The Warders had 20 bottles of wine and 40 rolls, ye Gunners 3 bottles and rolls and each boy a pint of ale and a roll. Ten pounds are allowed by the Government towards this (Preston, page 154).

Sadly, not all traditions are handed down!

Ceremony of the Lilies and the Roses

A ceremony instituted as recently as 1923 commemorates, and mourns, the murder of Henry VI in the Tower of London in

1471. Having lost his crown to Edward IV, Henry was imprisoned in the Wakefield Tower, and whilst at prayer he was brutally slain. He had been a pious and scholarly king, and had founded two of our great seats of learning – Eton College and King's College, Cambridge.

On the evening of 21 May each year, the anniversary of his death, representatives of the provosts of the two colleges join the Chaplain and a small party of yeoman warders in State Dress. A sheaf of three Eton lilies, tied with Eton blue ribbon, is laid on the spot where the king is believed to have fallen, together with white roses bound in mauve ribbon from King's College, Cambridge. Prayers are read by the Chaplain, and Henry VI's Latin prayer is sung, followed by a blessing. The flowers are left there for twenty-four hours, then removed and burnt.

Installation of the Constable

As mentioned earlier, the office of Constable of the Tower is one of great honour, carrying with it the privilege of direct communication with the sovereign. The first Constable was appointed in 1078, and in this century many distinguished soldiers have held this high office.

The Installation Ceremony itself takes place every five years and dates back to 1707. It is a ceremony of great significance and splendour, as it authorises the Constable to assume the responsibility for the Royal Palace and Fortress, and allows him to meet his men, the Body of Yeoman Warders.

Troops of regiments associated with the Constable's army service are the first to parade on Tower Green, then come other troops connected with the Tower. Next, as the band plays 'The Yeomen of England', the yeoman warders in State Dress march on with slow dignity to take up their positions in a circle inside the lines of soldiers. The Constable, the Resident Governor and the Chaplain then stand in the centre. The Queen's representative, the Lord Chamberlain arrives, to be greeted by the royal salute on the trumpets, and the royal letter appointing the Constable is read out. The Lord Chamberlain then delivers the gold Master Keys of the Tower to the Constable, saying, 'I have the honour, in the Queen's Name and on the Queen's behalf, to hand to you the Keys of the Tower of London and to charge you with the custody of the Tower itself'. The Chief

Warder then cries 'God Preserve Queen Elizabeth!' and all the warders shout 'Amen!'.

After the Chaplain has blessed the proceedings, the Keys, on a crimson velvet cushion, are carried by the Chief Warder ahead of the Constable, around the line of yeoman warders so that they can see the Keys and to allow the Constable to inspect the body of men he now commands. When the other troops have also been inspected and the occupancy of the Queen's House has been granted by the Constable to the Resident Governor, the band and trumpeters play as the parade marches off, bringing a spectacular and traditional ceremony to an end.

7 Living in the Tower

Would ye live in a palace or favour the cot
That circumstance argued should be your lot?
Would ye suffer the arrowslit's sliver of light
When ye yearned to lean forth and study the night?
Would ye settle to sleep at the turn of a key
Knowing only the moon is floating free?
 If all these things are within thy power
 Then ye'll be as one with Gundulf's Tower.

To the tourists the Tower is a museum. To the yeoman warders who live there with their families, it is home, a medieval village in the very heart of London. Even when the Tower was full of prisoners, many condemned to await the axe and others suffering close confinement, life for the staff went on as in any other village, with no less compassion than in communities adjacent to our prisons today. Warders and their families held their birthday parties and wedding feasts within the Tower, daughters flirted with the garrison soldiers and sons ogled the serving wenches in the coffee house. All led their own lives even while the great events on their doorstep were moulding the nation's history.

So it is today, on a different scale, and, as in every village, there is a squire, the Resident Governor, who lives in the big house on the village green, the Queen's House on Tower Green. At Christmas time he and his wife invite the Tower residents to a party in the richly panelled rooms of that historic Tudor house, and on the rare occasions that the City experiences snow, the children build snowmen in the moat and slide down the slopes. They enjoy themselves, unlike the ravens, who just can't understand it!

In the autumn a harvest festival is held in the village church, the Chapel Royal of St Peter ad Vincula. The guild of master bakers presents superbly fashioned plaques of bread to adorn the altar, alongside fruit and food for the less fortunate. And as befits the place where Guy Fawkes and his fellow conspirators were imprisoned and interrogated, on 5 November each year the yeoman warders and their families celebrate with a bonfire and fireworks in the moat, and refreshments prepared by the wives.

So the Tower has its private life. The postman and milkman make their daily rounds, the resident doctor holds evening surgeries. A village inn is of course essential, and while at one time the Tower boasted three taverns, the King's Head, the Golden Chain and the Cold Harbour, there is now only one, the Yeoman Warders' Club, surely one of the most exclusive clubs in London, having but thirty-nine members. And all patriotic villages have a flagpole: the one on the White Tower flies the largest union flag of any public building in the country, measuring 12ft (3.6m) by 21ft (6.4m). In winter a smaller flag is used.

Until some years ago the Tower village had its very own fire brigade and police force – it still has plenty of cells! In the grassed moat are a bowling green, swings and a tennis court, though in the two world wars, chicken runs and vegetable allotments flourished there. In one area of the moat, near Traitors' Gate, little gravestones mark the burial places of domestic pets which belonged to Victorian warders. Although at one time a school existed within the walls, the children now go to local schools. The wives, incidentally, find that their unusual residence isn't always such a novelty. Shop assistants, cashiers and taxi drivers find it hard to accept that their address is Her Majesty's Tower of London, and many an explanation is necessary to convince the sceptic. The crowds queueing for entrance to the grounds resent anyone walking past them and straight in, and the explanation 'I live here!' is futile and provokes many a ribald rejoinder. And to get to their houses while laden with shopping, especially if spiral stairs are blocked by tourists, isn't easy. It is not the visitors' fault, they just do not know – so I hope this book will enlighten them! And when the waiting crowds point at washing hanging on lines on the battlements to dry, well, that's the habit of centuries, except that it used to be doublets, not singlets!

So life in the Tower isn't easy. Dwellings (for which rent is paid) are small, with light admitted via arrowslits, and hemmed in by 40ft (12m) high walls, but the knowledge that one is living where Henry feasted and Richard cursed, where Elizabeth walked the ramparts and Mary brought her Spanish consort, compensates for everything. To walk round the Tower at night is to enter a stone time-machine. Every niche is full of memories, every building a backdrop for some historic figure who has shaped the nation's destiny or died for his principles. Once the surging crowds have gone, the Tower becomes its true self, a castellated mirror of the past, and to experience that atmosphere is reward indeed.

Living conditions in the old days were of course far worse, when hygiene was unknown and the effects of the evilly polluted moat filled the Tower's hospital. Closets were poised over the moat, and on 7 March 1733 it was reported that 'a poor soldier while on duty on the north wall, the box and house of easement [a lovely name for a toilet!] fell down into the moat with the poor fellow in it, which so bruised him that he never spoke, and dyed in two hours after' (Fox, page 81).

Another undesirable feature was the Royal Menagerie, described in a later chapter. The animal noises and smells of its elephant and bears, lions and leopards, could hardly have made the Tower a fresh and peaceful place to live. It all must have been enough to drive one to drink, a frequent remedy for everything in those times, and many warders spent far too long in the taverns. Warder Meret died through drinking too often with the yeoman porter and it despatched him to his grave in 1733. Two years earlier, Warder John Smith 'died of hard drinking, he was a Strong man and might have lived to a hundred had he not besotted himself', as the report on him noted (Fox, page 69).

The soldiers of the garrison also drank to excess at times, people 'selling them spiritous liquers from which arises many Irregularites and Disorderly Behaviours contrary to the good discipline of Old Soldiers, particularly at the period when the outposts are liable to be attacked by the enemy' – this was in March 1799 when the French threatened the nation's security (source unknown). Officers and men were forbidden to sell such drinks 'whereby soldiers may get Intoxicated. Those acting Contrary to this Order shall be tried by Court Martial and punished in a most Exemplary Manner' (source unknown). And in the following year, the daily issue of three pints of small beer per man was withdrawn. This was replaced by an allowance of a penny a day instead, known as beer money.

A favourite haunt of the warders was the old Tiger Tavern, now rebuilt and modernised, adjacent to the Tower. It is recorded in the Tower Records that as a protest against rationing and post-war restrictions:

His Honour the Lord Mayor of London did, on 19 December 1949, meet the Chief Warder and three yeoman warders at the West Gate of the Tower. They escorted him to the Tiger Tavern where, after appropriate speeches, the Lord Mayor raised above the door of the inn an Ale Garland to signify to all not only that good ale awaited the guests within, but that the Citizens of London one and all proclaim their defiance of the rigours and vexations of the times, and their will to stand fast for the upholding of the might, the unity and the weal of this Realm.

A declaration which no doubt was toasted with great fervour afterwards.

In the eighteenth century there was even a song (anon.) entitled 'Song of the Jolly Beef eating Warders'.

With my back to the fire and my paunch to the table,
Let me eat, let me drink as long as I'm able,
Let me eat, let me drink what e'er I set my whims on
'Til my nose is blue and my jolly visage crimson.
The doctor preaches abstinence and threatens me with dropsy,
But such advice, I needn't say, from drinking never stops ye,
The man who likes good liquor is of nature brisk and brave, boys,
So drink away! Drink while ye may! There's no drinking in the Grave, boys!

In those early days, warders, like their noble betters, were buried in or around the Chapel Royal of St Peter; William Thimbleby in September 1673, Jim Sparrowhawke in August 1681, not forgetting John Tudor who, after serving as a yeoman warder for over sixty years, died in September 1758 aged 107! Nowadays, warders must retire much earlier, but they still have the privilege of having their children and grandchildren christened and married in the chapel royal, their names being entered in the registers which record so many other, far more historic names and titles, for the record of christenings begins in 1587 and that of marriages in 1586.

There has always been a close link between the royal family and the Body of Yeoman Warders. In 1978, to celebrate the nine-hundredth anniversary of the Tower, Her Majesty the Queen and Prince Philip paid us a royal visit. After inspecting the yeoman warders, the royal guests were photographed with them and then took tea with the warders and their families in a marquee set up beside the White Tower. This informal relationship has grown up over the centuries, doubtless commencing with the warder's small son who, it is believed, gave Princess Elizabeth posies of flowers as she walked around the grounds during her imprisonment in 1554.

In the 1920s, King George V and Queen Mary often visited the Tower and were treated like much respected grandparents by the warders' children. Following the publication of my book *Ghosts of the Tower of London* in 1980, I received a long letter from Mr G.D. Trott. His father, George Trott RVM DCM, was Curator of the Crown Jewels from 1921 to 1951, and the younger George lived in the Tower from 1921 until leaving to join the Royal Air Force in 1936. I am indebted to him for the fascinating account that follows, and which I quote verbatim.

What stands out for me is when everyone was in their best dress with all wearing their medals, as when HRH the Prince of Wales presented the leeks to the Welsh Guards, and the greatest of them all when HM George V and Queen Mary visited us all. It was grand.

Various houses had been cleaned up and painted for Queen Mary to inspect but she would have none of it. She wanted to inspect the places *she* wanted to see. What a to-do! All the high-ups got upset about it, she really went to town about the conditions in which people lived. Afterwards nearly all the living quarters were cleaned and painted, etc.

What had happened was this. My mother and Mrs Smoker, the Chief Warder's wife, and the ladies of the Mothers' Union and Womens' Fellowship a few weeks earlier had been invited to tea at Buckingham Palace and Queen Mary had asked them about life in the 'Bloody Tower' as she called *all* the Tower of London. The ladies told her about life there and all about us children.

So when she came she knew all about it. She also told the ladies not to say a word until after the visit. When she came to talk to the children she asked for various boys and girls and one of them was me. When she spoke to me with her charming accent (I forget what she said) I gave her a kind of saucy answer and she told me to turn round and gave me a whack with her umbrella for being saucy and told me she would tell my mother, which she did! – and I got put to bed without any supper, early. Those were the Happy Days in the Tower.

At various times members of the Royal Family would come to visit the Tower with friends, not official visits, so my father and the yeoman warders got to know them quite well.

On one occasion I took a jug of tea to my father in the Wakefield Tower (then the Jewel House) and the Chief Warder and Yeoman Gaoler with two yeoman warders were outside, and the Chief Warder, Mr Smoker, called up to my dad and I was told to come up.

So when I got to the top of the stairs I took the jug of tea into the little room and went into the Jewel Chamber and only a few persons were there, my father, Major General Sir George Younghusband, Keeper of the Crown Jewels, together with a gentleman who I believe was Lord Chamberlain Lord Atholl, and HM George V (in civvies). He had come to see the Crowns, etc, regarding their cleaning by the Royal Jewellers. I took off my school cap and bowed. He spoke to me and said 'I remember you' and he told my dad and the others how he had met me and some of the children of the Royal Mews when he had visited the Mews some time before. My mother had taken me and some of the Tower children to see a lady whose husband was a groom at the Palace; when we children went into the Palace grounds we had met His Majesty whom we thought was a gardener of the Palace.

Another event was about Mr and Mrs Grost, American friends of Mrs Simpson (who later married King Edward VIII). My cousin, Reg Best, was Mr Grost's chauffeur, and he once parked the car outside our house in the Tower and introduced Mrs Grost and Mrs Simpson to my mother. He then took them up to the Jewel House, which had been cleared except for my father and two yeoman warders. Sir George Younghusband had had a phone call from the Palace from the King (Edward VIII) to show them round. My mother told me afterwards that Mrs Simpson had wanted my father to point out which crown the Queen would wear. We often wondered about that.

If a baby was born in the Tower or the mother and father had lived in the Tower, the news was given to the Constable and he informed the Monarch who would send back greetings. The yeoman warders would invite the father to a drink and later on the Mothers' Union and Womens' Fellowship would give a tea party for the mother and baby, with gifts from all the families. The event would be recorded by the Chief Warder in the records kept in the Resident Governor's House.

I remember going up with three of the warders' sons to see my father take the Crown Jewels out of the Cage, he had to take his boots off so as to keep to the regulations, because of all the carpeting. He handed the Crown Jewels out to the three yeoman warders, Sprake, Drake and Phillips, and the Chief Warder, Mr Smoker. They then handed them to the Crown Jewellers.

After a while one of the men put one of the crowns on his head, and it ended up with everyone trying on all the crowns. Then they put them on us young lads, what a big laugh they all had because the crowns came down right over our eyes!

Not a practice that would be permitted now, with or without one's boots on!

During the last war, of course, the regalia and jewels were moved to a place of safety for the duration of hostilities. The Tower was closed to the public, though servicemen were admitted – indeed, over three-quarters of all American troops in the country visited the Tower. Wartime life within the walls was arduous. Some warders rejoined the services, others retired at the age limit, leaving only twenty-two available for duty. The constant air raids on London caused much bomb damage to the ancient buildings, the North Bastion on the outer wall receiving a direct hit. Its occupant, Yeoman Warder S. Reeves was killed, a risk all warders and their families took as they coped with incendiary and high-explosive bombs.

However, in 1945 the public were welcomed back, the damage was repaired and the Body of Yeoman Warders was once more restored to full strength.

8 On the Wharf

Go walk on the wharf and ye'll surely see
The world and his wife and children three.
Dogs in assortment, beggars leering,
Office boys fresh from a nearby beering,
Pink at the collar and daft at the knees
All set for a wench or two to tease.

But go again in a silent hour
When the cobbles are wet from an evening shower,
Ye'll see how the silvery shaft of the moon
Glints on the tiny buckled shoon
Of my lady who hurries her lord to see,
For a prisoner so in the Tower is he.

Although nowadays it is little more than an pleasant short-cut by the river, or a place where weary tourists can sit and have a picnic, the Tower Wharf is, nevertheless, as steeped in history as the fortress itself. At one time or another during its seven centuries of existence, it has experienced a zoo at one end and gun manufactories at the other. Between the two, the royal barges moored, while beneath the Wharf other boats brought the doomed prisoners into captivity.

On the Wharf, rows of cannon defended London, and escaping prisoners fled across it – even Colonel Blood ran along its cobbles, dropping some of the precious stones he had stolen. Many famous captives have gazed down longingly at the Wharf's promise of freedom: Sir Walter Raleigh from the Bloody Tower, Guy Fawkes through the windows of the Lieutenant's Lodgings. And from the battlements adjoining the Bell Tower, Princess Elizabeth (who later became Queen Elizabeth I) had a full view of the river, the Wharf and the City when imprisoned by her half sister Queen Mary.

Great ships have anchored off the Wharf's reaches, from Tudor men-of-war to modern battle cruisers. It has felt the impact of enemy missiles: stone shot hurled across the river by Yorkist trebuchets in 1460, shrapnel from high-explosive bombs in World War II. Small railways once traversed it, and the river's edge was lined with derricks – hoists shaped like gallows and named after Derrick, the executioner who despatched Queen Elizabeth's favourite, Robert Devereux Earl of Essex, to his death on Tower Green within the walls.

So it is no ordinary stretch of ground. Built on the orders of Henry III on land reclaimed from the River Thames, it was constructed by the sinking of hundreds of tree trunks vertically into the earth. Rocks and more earth were added to form the foundation for the roadway, the riverside wall being faced with stone to resist the erosion of the waters. A short tunnel beneath the Wharf, still visible though bricked up against the fast-flowing river, admitted boats carrying prisoners through Traitors' Gate. This water-gate was protected by a portcullis, a vertically sliding door operated from St Thomas's Tower above; and through the arrowslits each side of the forbidding archway, the prisoners could be identified and closely observed without being able to see their future gaolers.

On other parts of the Wharf, dwelling houses were built for occupation by yeoman warders and Tower officials. In 1439 Elyngham, Keeper of the King's Tents, was granted 6d (2½p) a day, a suit of the uniform of the Yeomen of the Wardrobe 'new every Christmas from Christmas next' (Calendar of Patent Rolls, Henry VI), and a house on the Wharf with the adjacent garden one hundred feet in length.

The royal families of course disembarked on the Wharf itself, coming ashore at the King's Steps, which can still be seen at the westerly end of the embankment. Opposite the steps was their private entrance, the Byward Sally Port, which bypassed the challenges and identity checks faced by ordinary visitors. Still surviving across the narrow part of the moat between the Byward Tower and the Wharf, is the little sliding drawbridge. This was operated by means of the large iron wheel beside it, and was doubtless the responsibility of the Yeoman Porter. To ensure that only those who were entitled actually entered by that route, a sentry was stationed within. Visitors even now will notice a sentry box still in position, and indeed a soldier stands night guard facing the Sally Port entrance.

As the fortress was for centuries the nation's military arsenal, facilities were necessary for bringing in raw materials and supplies, and for despatching ordnance and weapons, ammunition and stores for use in foreign wars. Roads and vehicles being inadequate, the river thus provided the main transport route, and strings of barges and fleets of sailing ships constantly moored alongside the Wharf, creating a scene of continual activity. At one time a small railway ran via a tunnel into the basement of the White Tower, and gangs of porters ferried supplies to and from the many workshops, forges and storerooms within the walls.

For over three hundred years the Tower was not only an arms depot, but also a factory producing thousands of guns a year, and long sheds were erected along the east end of the Wharf to house the workmen and machines. Other buildings sprang up around them – stables and coach-houses, and the workplaces of carpenters and wheelwrights, farriers and stonemasons. In the seventeenth century, equipment was set up in St Thomas Tower above Traitors' Gate, a 'water engine' being installed in the pool beneath. This was powered by the tide or by horse power, and it pumped water up to the huge tanks on top of the White Tower. Later it was replaced by a steam engine, which could also drive machinery making gun barrels.

Ordnance continued to be made in the Tower until early in the last century, when the large numbers of more advanced armaments simply could not be manufactured in the Tower's limited area. Military hardware, Tudor style and of other ages, is still on display of course, in what is accepted as one of the finest arms and armour museums in the world.

Another great showpiece at the Tower, and one which attracted not only the public but members of royal families of every reign, was the Royal Menagerie. This was situated at the extreme west end of the Wharf and was started in 1235 with a gift of three leopards from Emperor Frederick II to King Henry III. From then on the zoo grew rapidly.

A white bear arrived and, tethered by a chain, was allowed to fish in the Thames; its keeper was paid 4d a day. Later, King Louis of France presented an elephant – 'most seldome or never any of that kind had beene seene in England before that time' (Holinshed's Chronicles) – and it was joined by lions, tigers and many exotic birds. Ration money for the big cats was set at 6d (2½p) a day each, with 1½d for their keepers, but by the fourteenth century Berenger Candrer, Keeper of the Lions and Leopards, was getting over 3s (15p) a day. This appointment, plus that of Master of the King's Bears and Apes, frequently became another perquisite of the Constable or Lieutenant, the actual work being delegated to a deputy, though not all the income!

James I took a great personal interest in his menagerie, ordering fights to the death between lions and dogs, bear-baiting and similar barbaric spectacles for his entertainment. On one occasion a child, entering the bear house, was killed by the animal, whereupon the king decreed that the bear be baited to death. This public attraction brought in so much money that £20 of it was awarded to the mother of the child, in compensation.

Lions have always held a fascination for royalty, as well they might. James, Duke of Monmouth, offered to enter a lion's cage as evidence of his royal descent. It was common knowledge, he averred, that lions would never attack one of such noble blood. And in 1775 a soldier who encountered two African natives with a captured lion, killed the men and brought the lion to England, where he presented it to George III. The beast was put in the Tower menagerie and the soldier was granted discharge from the army and given a pension of £50 a year for life.

At the height of its popularity in the 1820s, the zoo boasted over sixty specimens of animals and birds, many of them caged in the Lion Tower, a semicircular bastion near the main gates, the others in additional buildings nearby. Bears, lions, tigers, leopards and hyenas all made a visit to the Tower Wharf worthwhile, with porcupines, sea eagles, pelicans and alligators as extra attractions.

Regrettably, however, the very success of the menagerie spelt its demise. The animal houses and pens impeded entrance to the Tower and in 1834 their occupants were transferred to form the London Zoo in Regent's Park. By 1850 the buildings had been demolished, though for some time afterwards gullible members of the public were victims of a confidence trick, buying tickets to see the Annual Washing of the Lions, scheduled for 1 April each year, of course. On one particular occasion, in response to hoax advertisements placed in the London papers, vast crowds assembled at the gates to watch the spectacle, while queues of hansom-cabs and horse-drawn buses blocked Tower Hill for hours. Such was, and is, the public's suspicion that those in authority seek to deprive them of a treat, that it took all the persuasive powers of the yeoman warders there to disperse them. Duty at the main gate was never easy.

Nor was duty at the East Gate, by St Katherine's Dock. During the last century in particular, living conditions for most of the inhabitants of the East End were squalid and primitive. Housed in slums which lacked everything but the most basic facilities, surviving on inadequate wages and resigned to a future that held nothing but misery, many ended it all in the river, their corpses floating on the tide by the Tower Wharf. It was then the unpleasant task of the Chief Warder, on opening up the Wharf gates early in the morning, to pull the bodies ashore using the implement which still exists in the Tower: three sharp, curved grappling hooks, surmounting a very long pole. After 1894, the bodies were kept temporarily in a stone vault under Tower Bridge, a cold and eerie chamber as I can vouch for from personal inspection. The vault was called 'Dead Man's Hole', and a notice to that effect is fixed to the wall by the stairs at the north end of the bridge.

One of the great royal events of the last hundred years to take place on the Wharf was the official opening of Tower Bridge on 30 June 1894. Compared to the Tower of London, the bridge's mortar isn't dry yet, but it deserves a place in this book because of its proximity and also the fascination it holds for foreign tourists, many of whom are convinced that it is London Bridge or even part of the castle itself. The last bridge before the open sea, it literally towers over the Tower, the high walkway being 142ft (43m) above high-water level.

Sir John Wolfe Barry, the engineer, created a masterpiece of steel and stone – granite covering a steel skeleton. It took eight years to build and cost nearly £1 million. It is just starting to show its age, and credit is due to those who in 1878 designed it to carry traffic which was mainly horse-drawn, slow and leisurely. The specifications it had to meet were a blend of Victorian common sense and tradition. The bascules of the opening roadway, weighing a thousand tons each, should resemble in their action the drawbridges of the adjacent castle. The turrets should be in aesthetic harmony with the Tower's turrets. In the event of an attack on the Tower of London, the military would control the commanding heights by mounting guns at the top of the bridge, and indeed an anti-aircraft battery was installed there in World War II.

When all the international merchant shipping visited the

The official opening of Tower Bridge by HRH The Prince of Wales, 30 June 1894. Note the Life Guards lined up on the left of the Wharf

upper pool of London, the bridge had to remain open for two hours every high tide, with pedestrians using the lifts and high walkway. To avoid delays in opening, stables on the bridge supplied fresh horses to assist slow-moving wagons to clear the bascules. And should a sailing ship be becalmed underneath, a boat was always positioned nearby to drag it clear so that the bascules could be lowered again.

Repairs on the underside of the structure still have to be indicated by a lamp at night and a handful of straw by day; and although the walkway, which was high enough to permit the passage of the tallest warship, was closed in 1911, it has recently been re-opened to the public, thus providing a magnificent vista of London and its river.

The official opening of the bridge was a great day for the City. The Tower Wharf had been spring-cleaned, its cannons re-painted, its turf close-clipped. Marquees were set up along its length, with viewing platforms and stands erected for the high-ranking spectators. The Upper Pool, the stretch of river between London Bridge and the Tower Bridge, was a bobbing mass of small boats, many chartered for the day, filled with Londoners celebrating the birth of a London landmark. Hundreds of their fellow citizens lined the banks of the river, leaning from warehouse windows and rooftops. East of the new bridge, scores of sailing vessels, launches and paddle-steamers, dressed overall with flags and brightly coloured bunting, jostled for position to pass through on this the first real opening of the bascules.

On land, too, the City had prepared for the royal procession. All traffic had been cleared from the route, and the streets had been cleaned and decorated with triumphal arches and more flags everywhere. At eleven o'clock HRH the Prince of Wales, accompanied by the Princess, the Duke of York and other members of the royal family, left Marlborough House. Passing St Paul's Cathedral, they moved through cheering crowds along East Cheap and Byward Street to the Tower. There all was ready, the yeoman warders in their State Dress and the Life-guards lined up along the Wharf, their horses restive with the atmosphere of mounting excitement. The royal party were met at the entrance to the Wharf by the Constable of the Tower, General Sir Daniel Lysons, who, with the Chief Warder, escorted them to the bridge.

In the control room the officials were introduced to His Royal Highness, who then operated the levers controlling the great steam engines installed on the southern approach road. As he did so, the prince declared the bridge open, and to the accompaniment of deafening cheers, steam whistles and the sounds of rattles and bells, the great bascules lifted majestically. Simultaneously, the guns of the Tower boomed out, smoke billowing across the water and the echoes reverberating from the warehouses opposite and resounding throughout the City. The Prince of Wales then boarded the steam yacht *Palm* and, joined by the waiting flotilla, passed under the bridge, leading a gaily bedecked procession while the massed crowds waved from shore and rooftop, tower and turret. Sailing past the Tower of London, the *Palm* proceeded beneath London Bridge, saluting the thousands of spectators, and sailed onwards upriver to Westminster Pier, where the royal party disembarked.

So Tower Wharf has, through the ages, seen it all. Where lions once roared, the public now buy souvenirs and postcards. In the archway through which Elizabeth I's carriage rattled over the cobbles, tourists hand their tickets to the yeoman warder on duty. Sightseers high on Raleigh's Walk look down to view litter bins and snack bars by the ancient cannon.

But no modernity can deprive the Tower and its Wharf of their memories, for the magic and mystery will always be there.

9 The Ravens

An Echo of Ravens it should be
To describe this bird collectively.
For if one doth croak
Thou canst swear on thy sword
That another one stands
Across the sward
Dipping and calling and gawkily hopping,
One wing outstretched – the other one dropping.
Fashioned like this with a few feathers clipped
So our Sovereign shall rule
And her Crown ne'er be tipped.

Yeoman warders and their families do not have the Tower of London all to themselves – they have to share it with a few very large birds who are just as well known. They are of course the ravens.

The medieval towns supported hundreds of these birds, nesting in the steeples and tall buildings, and finding plenty of rotting food to scavenge in the streets. Their presence in the Tower was mentioned in the reign of Henry VIII, and when the Royal Observatory was established in the round turret of the White Tower by Charles II, the Astronomer Royal complained bitterly about the mess made by the ravens. The king's order that they should be destroyed was cancelled, it is said, when he was informed of a legend to the effect that this would cause the White Tower to collapse and England to lose all her power and possessions.

It can only be assumed that the person who related this to the king had studied Celtic mythology, for therein lies the origin of the legend. Bran the Blessed, a god of the underworld, engaged his enemies in mortal combat. He was wounded in the foot by a poisoned arrow and, near to death, directed that his head should be cut off, taken to London and buried in the White Mount, meaning Tower Hill. The head was to face France, and as long as it remained buried, England would never be invaded. The significance becomes immediately apparent when it is realised that the name 'Bran' is Celtic for raven!

The birds were also revered by the Norsemen as the messengers of their gods, and were portrayed on battle standards by the fierce warriors from Norway and Denmark. So where is there a more fitting home for the ravens than in a castle built by the Nordic descendents, the Normans?

Charles II heeded the warning, and since then the birds have been a feature of the Tower. For many years, six have been on the official ration strength plus one or two in reserve. An allowance is paid for their food, which nowadays consists of raw meat, rabbit heads, fruit and eggs, and they are adept at extracting sandwiches from cellophane packs discarded by tourists. Destructive by nature, they pick at the putty in window frames and at the chapel royal's leaded lights. The birds will even use their sharp beaks on tourists' fingers and ankles. They do not breed in captivity but are obtained while young from Scotland, Wales and the West country. All are given names of course, Cora, Corax, Gunn, Garvie, Charles and Cronk being just a few.

One notable bird was Edgar Sopper, named thus by his ex-owner, Colonel Sopper. Edgar would visit the house above Traitors' Gate to be fussed over, but if he was not admitted promptly, he would toss plant pots down the steps! In April 1924 a raven called Jim Crow died at the grand old age of forty-four. Edgar observed the commotion this caused and so the next morning when the Resident Governor looked out of his window, he saw yet another dead raven, claws in the air, lying on Tower Green. Hastening out to the 'corpse', his sorrow turned to fury as Edgar, for he it was, bit the Governor smartly on the finger and flapped away, croaking triumphantly. Playing dead became quite a habit with him, the children gathering round to watch the performance.

When Tower ravens are finally summoned to the Great Litter Bin in the Sky, so to speak, they are buried in a grave set aside for them in the moat by the Middle Drawbridge. World War II caused casualties, two of their number being killed by enemy action. Then in 1946 Mabel, aged fourteen, mysteriously disappeared, believed kidnapped; and by the following year only one survived, sixteen-year old Grip. Later, however, more were recruited and the dreaded legend was thwarted.

The birds would of course fly away if possible, and indeed many years ago, one left the Tower and took up residence on St Paul's Cathedral, on religious grounds no doubt. Another, in 1889, took off and settled in Kensington Gardens. This tendency is curbed nowadays for they have a wing clipped, a painless operation which restricts their flying ability. They are fed and cared for by the Yeoman Ravenmaster, a warder who takes on the task in addition to his normal duties. A dedicated and conscientious keeper, he gets up early, summer and winter, to clean their cages by the Wakefield Tower, prepare their food and, when dusk approaches, to coax them back to their perches for the night. They know his voice of course, but being completely independent, will go to bed only when it suits them.

Other birds and domestic pets give them a wide berth. Seagulls warily bank away, and should a pigeon venture too close to a hungry raven, only a wide swathe of feathers will remain to mark the impromptu snack. As kings of the castle, ravens will not tolerate even the mention of larger birds. Just before the last war a visiting Nazi dignitary sneeringly remarked that in his country *they* had eagles. Whereupon the raven he was pointing at came over and bit him!

The birds have a superior air about them, almost as if they know the age-old secrets of the Tower – knowledge passed down to them by their forebears who witnessed the historic events within its walls. They invariably spend their time on the lawns in the central part of the Tower, the Inner Ward. That is their domain, near their birdbaths and where scraps of food are discarded by visitors. Rarely, if ever, do they venture into the casemates, the private area between the inner and outer encircling walls where most of the yeoman warders and their families live. But when warders were allowed to continue their duties until they died – rather than having to retire on reaching the age of sixty-five as now – instances occurred when the ravens lived up to their evil reputation of being precursors of death.

Mr Trott, who was quoted earlier, recalls a yeoman warder being taken ill. When his condition worsened, a raven left the Green and hopped down the steps, across the casemates and up on to the battlements of the outer wall above the warder's house. The Ravenmaster tried to entice it away but without success, until after the warder had died. Only then did it return to the Inner Ward. And when Mr Trott's mother passed away on 4 October 1950, he, with yeoman warders and their wives, heard the croaking of a raven on the roof. 'Leave him, he will soon go,' said Mr Trott's father, a prophesy which sadly was true.

Another strange incident occurred when a sentry shot himself by the Well Tower. Help was only forthcoming when Warders Sprake and Phillips heard a raven croaking loudly nearby, and it didn't leave the scene until the ambulance had departed. And in World War II, a raven was present when a German spy, Josef Jakobs, was executed by firing squad in an enclosed rifle range situated in the casemates. Just before the condemned man and his escort marched in, the raven came down the steps and stood croaking less than ten yards away. A senior officer tried to drive it away, but the warders present pointed out the futility of the attempt. It was not until the body had been removed to the Tower morgue that the raven rejoined his companions on the Green.

Even in recent years the birds have shown uncanny knowledge of impending disaster. Early one morning the Yeoman Gaoler and his wife saw a raven in the casemates, pecking at the tyres of their son's car. They were surprised at seeing a raven there but attached little significance to the incident. Later, on hearing that a transport strike prevented his usual mode of travel, their son decided to use his car. And as he drove over a crossroads another vehicle collided with him at speed, completely wrecking his car. Fortunately uninjured, he said afterwards that he never even saw the other car coming – but the raven knew!

10 Curiosities and Calamities

Safe are thy vows
Ever resting with me
Comic or cryptic
Repentant or free
Enter them here
Twixt one ear and the other
So none may divine we are rival or brother.

For a person with an enquiring mind, living in the Tower is a rich experience. Nearly everything in sight poses questions and invites research. Things constructed for reasons which were obvious centuries ago are still there, but the reasons aren't, and until curiosity is satisfied, the very buildings themselves seem to mock one's lack of knowledge.

Nor is curiosity limited to residents. Every day, vast numbers of tourists visit the Tower, looking everywhere with wondering eyes. On the assumption that the castle belongs to the yeoman warders, so to speak, they expect answers to their wondering questions. Why do the old spiral stairs wind clockwise on ascending? Why is the Middle Tower so called? Why is the moat so shallow? And as it is hard to admit ignorance, the reasons need to be sought. For the benefit of those who have been to the Tower and noticed oddities but never asked, or for those yet to pay a visit, an account of some of its past and present curiosities is included here.

Approaching the main entrance to the castle, all is modern, with tarmac, litter bins and ice-cream vans. But here and there on the pavement edge stand hollow iron bollards, painted black. These are old cannon, captured from the French in the Napoleonic Wars, and indeed some, sunk less deep than others, reveal at pavement level the swivel where they were attached to the gun carriages. Not many have survived traffic improvement schemes, but fifty years ago more than seventy lined the route up the steep slope from Billingsgate fish-market, past the Tower and on up to the main road at Tower Hill.

Whatever value these cannon were to Napoleon, they were invaluable to the fish-carters' horses! For centuries, fish of all kinds was sold at Billingsgate, daily deliveries being made to the City's shops, hotels and restaurants. These consignments, packed in ice, had to be fresh, and so the collection started well before dawn, with a minimum amount of time lost en route. The heavily laden carts would rattle over the slippery cobbles, horses straining up the gradient to the main road. When they ran out of breath or lost their footing, the carter would bring them to a halt and, rather than have his cart slither away out of control, would back his steeds until the tailboard butted against the nearest cannon. No precious ground lost, the horses given a breather, three cheers for Napoleon! This practice continued until well after World War II, when motorisation set in and the gradient ceased to be a problem.

Similar trophies may be found along Tower Wharf, and one unique specimen stands near the White Tower. To all appearances an ordinary, if elderly, street lamp, it actually consists of an iron tube, one end bearing the lamp fixture, the other end inserted down into the muzzle of a cannon. It is believed to be the only one of its kind in London, yet it hardly attracts a second glance from the tourists.

Traces of another war, later than Napoleon's, linger on the big front gates and railings. Close inspection will reveal the misshapen scars where metal was torn away by flying shrapnel from the high-explosive bombs dropped around the Tower during the last war. A sentry on duty at the front gate during an air raid was killed and many neighbouring buildings were destroyed. Other duty personnel patrolling the moat often took shelter in the alcoves still visible in its outer wall; these were once the outlets of the City's drains but are now bricked up.

The moat itself was originally much deeper than seen now. Its stagnant waters were so fetid and evil smelling that it was drained in 1843 on the orders of the Duke of Wellington, then Constable of the Tower, and the thick mud yielded many interesting artifacts, from bones to cannonballs. Cleaned out, the moat was then filled up with 15ft (10.5m) of oyster shells to provide good drainage and a foundation for turfing. A century or more ago oysters were the everyday food of the Londoners, being cheap and plentiful, and with Billingsgate fish-market near at hand, the required quantities of shells were easily forthcoming.

Crossing the moat entails passing through the archway of the Middle Tower, so called because it once stood in the middle of the moat, with a drawbridge on each side of it. The Middle Tower is set at right angles to the steep approach road, ensuring that attackers bearing battering rams would, by sheer momentum, plunge past and into the river. The inner drawbridge is now replaced by a causeway leading under the Byward Tower and skirting the Bell Tower. This thirteenth-century prison tower contains the castle's alarm and curfew bell within its white wooden belfry. Crowning the structure is a ball, in the top of which may just be seen a coin, pressed in vertically. This is a commemorative crown, which was placed there when the belfry was repaired in 1976.

Further along the roadway, called Water Lane because the river earlier washed against the inner encircling wall, the Bloody Tower looms. On the left-hand side of its archway, a large iron ring hangs, heavy and ancient. Before the outer wall was built in the thirteenth century, boats would be moored to this ring, their royal passengers stepping out on to the rising ground that led through the archway and into the castle proper.

Within the Bloody Tower and some of the others, the spiral or well stairs twist clockwise ascending. Not without a good reason, for a right-handed defender thereby had tremendous advantage over an attacker who, in mounting the stairs, had to wield his sword 'round the corner'. Left-handed attackers must have been much sought after. A further peril for the unwary lurks on the Bloody Tower spiral. One step about halfway up is twice the depth of the others. For a person escaping down the stairs, this sudden and unexpected drop turns flight into a headlong descent, the rough stone walls providing neither handhold nor cushion.

There is something very satisfying about seeing dates on structures, and the Tower possesses quite a few, not all of them easily spotted. At the top of the drain-pipes around the outer walls above the moat, the hopper heads (collector boxes) bear the letters VR and the date 1843 in gold paint, whereas those high on the east and west walls of the White Tower boast 1709 AR, from the reign of Anne Regina. The immense lead flower-boxes which stand on Tower Green and near the New

Armouries have GRI 1719 and GRII 1729 on their sides, together with the royal coat of arms; and the fountain on the Green, so popular with the tourists during heat waves, is dated 1913 GRV.

As a reminder of the days when much of the nation's ordnance was made and stored in the Tower, many bracketed wall lamps bear the ordnance badge of three cannon, one above the other. On the side wall of the New Armouries is mounted a magnificently carved coat of arms, that of George III, dating back to about 1800.

The Tower has long been the source of popular sayings, some more macabre than others. In 1660 the Lieutenant of the Tower was Sir John Robinson, and a condemned prisoner, on asking his warder if his execution would be quick, was reassured with the words: 'The axe goes up – comes down – and your head's off before you can say "Jack Robinson"!' (source unknown). 'Get it in the neck', referring to the axe, is painfully obvious, while 'Gone West' recalls the trip from the Tower to Tyburn, the public execution site. 'In the cart' was where the victim stood, rope around his neck, dreading the vehicle's abrupt departure. The origin of a more pleasant saying can actually be seen in the White Tower. Along a wall hangs a row of brimless metal bowls – protective headgear designed to be worn under soft Cavalier-type hats. The name of the metal bowl is a 'secret', hence 'Keep it under your hat'!

In front of the White Tower is the Waterloo Block; this replaced the Grand Storehouse which was burnt down in 1841. The Storehouse, a very imposing building, was officially opened by King William and Queen Mary in 1692 and a royal banquet was held. Among those attending were the masons and work-men wearing their traditional white aprons and gloves. One of the same trade, perhaps years earlier, engraved the masonic emblem in a large flat stone only yards from the Beauchamp Tower, visible to all but noticed by only a few.

One would think that, after nine centuries, everything about the Tower would have been discovered (except Barkstead's treasure!), but this is far from being the case. Cleaning, restoring and digging even now reveals long hidden objects, some of beauty, others of more sinister implication.

Workmen digging on the east side of the White Tower in 1772 discovered a small jewelled crown set with emeralds, rubies and pearls; it was dirt encrusted and heavily tarnished after years, perhaps centuries, underground. Much later, in 1953, while renovation was taking place in an upper chamber of the Byward Tower, a fourteenth-century religious mural was uncovered, showing that the room had been used as a medieval chapel. Similarly, nine years later, a gloriously carved sixteenth-century timbered ceiling saw light of day in the Council Chamber within the Queen's House and is now restored to its former glory. The building itself was for decades coated with grey plaster until restoration revealed the Tudor frontage seen today.

Digging, whether for pipe laying or foundations, nearly always provides a harvest. Anything from oyster shells to musket balls and clay pipes to human bones are likely to appear. When the Jewel House was being built, the initial excavation in March 1964 uncovered the remains of a number of bodies, which were then reverently placed in an oak casket. A brass plate giving details was attached, and the casket was interred in the crypt of the chapel royal nearby. And in 1976, workmen in a trench 15ft (4.5m) down at the base of the Roman wall, came across a complete skeleton. It lay in a short grave, with knees raised, and its tilted skull bore a gaping hole. The remains were taken away and, after much examination, were dated as being from about AD70.

Not all bones were buried and forgotten, however. The Royal Mint, manufacturing the nation's coinage for hundreds of years in the Tower, certainly found a use for some. Many of its employees, exposed in their work to the mingled and poisonous fumes of arsenic and sulphur rising from the crucibles, contracted acute sickness and disease. They were therefore granted a unique privilege, that of claiming the bleached skulls of those whose heads had been exhibited on Traitors' Gate, for it was a proven fact that any medicine drunk from a dead man's skull was doubly effective. Alas, 'though men dranke and some found relief, most of them died and it availed nought against the pestilence' (Stow's Annals, Vol II).

References to secret underground passages appear in many old books, from tunnels to convey prisoners from the Queen's House to the torture room in the White Tower basement, to passages passing under the moat and into long gone vaults of Tudor houses. Their existence is doubtful, for lack of evidence, though traces of some are occasionally found, going only a few yards before being blocked by earth falls. Sometimes old cellars are found under towers, filled with rubble, shards of pottery and old bottles. After extensive study by the skilled archaeologist Mr Geoffrey Parnell and his colleagues, much useful information is gleaned about the dates of the artifacts and the way of life in the Tower at the time.

By all accounts, it must have been as eventful in the old days as it is now, though in rather different ways. In the bitterly cold winter of 1728 a cormorant perched on a White Tower turret. When shot down, it was found to have its tail feathers frozen together by a piece of ice the size of a large walnut. The bird was sent to Sir Hans Sloane, King's Physician and President of the Royal Society, who identified and dissected it.

A few years later an official of the Mint was bitten by a mad dog whilst in the Tower. Despite the fashionable remedy of being immersed in salt water several times, he died, with all the symptoms of madness. All dogs were then killed or put out of the Tower 'except those of Gentlemen or Ladys, which were ordered to be tyed up'. Not altogether an effective measure, for three months later it was reported by the Deputy Lieutenant that 'A mad dog bit a poor sailor in the leg in the Tower, I ordered him to be immediately shot which was don accordingly' (Fox, page 81). It is assumed that the order referred to the dog and not the poor sailor.

In 1796, whilst the echoes of the French Revolution were still causing nervous apprehension amongst members of the government in this country, a feeling almost of terror must have spread through the wealthier of the City's inhabitants when, on a bright January day, a huge tricolour flag of the French republic suddenly appeared at the Tower. This feared symbol of the revolutionaries was seen draped over the battlements, and over two hours elapsed before the authorities became aware of it. The Major of the Tower, Colonel Matthew Smith, and his men, mounted the ramparts, only to find that the flag had been taken down. It was then reported to have reappeared further along the walls, and the irate major continued his chase, which only ended some time later when the flag was discovered under the bed of the miscreant, the fifteen-year-old son of the deputy chaplain. History books of the time draw a discreet veil over the punishment handed out.

A curiosity exhibited for many years in the Tower attracted much comment from foreign visitors, and rightly so, for it was nothing less than a unicorn's horn. In 1634 it was said to be worth £20,000 sterling, and so was kept in the Lower Jewel

House. One tourist, who had previously inspected the horn shown in St Marks, Venice, and another on display in a Paris museum, had become something of an expert on them. He declared that a horn was white when taken from the unicorn's head, so the yellow one in the Tower was at least a hundred years old. Whether it would eventually turn black, let others decide, he concluded. A further estimate of this exhibit's value was made in 1641 by no less exalted a personage than the Marquis de la Ferte Imbaut, Marshal of France. The horn was by then decorated with plates of silver, and the marshal valued it at £40,000, a king's ransom in those days. If one were available today, who'd queue to see the Crown Jewels?

Because of the Tower's great age, it has been subjected to many calamities of one sort or another, natural or man-made, though many of the earlier ones went unrecorded. Being situated by the River Thames, the castle was always vulnerable to flooding, high tides surging over the Wharf and pouring into the moat. On at least three occasions, in November 1833, January 1928 and February 1953, sentries had to make a rapid departure from their beat as water rushed through archways, flooding cellars and storerooms. Despite increasing the height of the river wall, the risk has always been there, only now removed by the completion of the Thames Barrier.

And if it wasn't too much water coming in, it was too much water going out. The sluice gates under Traitors' Gate were far from efficient, and in March 1558 there was a record low tide, the river ebbing until 'men myght stand in the mydes of Tames' (source unknown). This almost drained the moat, requiring security to be increased lest prisoners were tempted to escape.

Heavy frosts caused similar problems, and on several occasions the river froze over completely. In 1093 horses and wagons were able to travel from bank to bank, while in 1537 the ice was so thick that Henry VIII and Jane Seymour, accompanied by members of the Court, rode across on horseback. But the greatest frost of all started early in January 1684 and lasted into the following month. The Tower families joined in the festivities on the new playground, shopping at the scores of booths set up on the ice. Coaches plied for hire past the frozen entrance to Traitors' Gate, and the warders' children skated out to the vessels locked in the ice near Tower Wharf.

The Great Frost, as it was called, brought hardship in its wake. Water supplies were almost unobtainable in the Tower, owing to frozen pipes and tanks, and so cold were the thick walls of the castle buildings that fuel became scarce. As there was little or no wind, a pall of black choking smoke from the City's domestic fires hung over London for days, so that one 'could hardly see acrosse streets, it filling the lungs with its grosse particles so that one could hardly breath' (Diary, John Evelyn).

Just as frosts and floods assailed the Tower, so did storms, especially the Great Storm of November 1703 when unusually high tides coincided with severe gales. Downriver no fewer than seven hundred sailing ships were scattered, boats dashed to pieces and ferries driven under and into the bridge supports. Over three hundred seamen were believed drowned, many from the long strings of laden barges which broke up and sank in the wild waves and the darkness. Around the coasts twelve warships sank, as did scores of merchant ships, and many hundreds of mariners were lost.

The City fared badly in the gales which persisted for several days, flimsy dwellings collapsing and roofs being torn off. In the Tower, the fine Tudor houses adjoining the Lieutenant's Lodgings on Tower Green were blown down. Not only did Yeoman Warder John Bull lose his home, but a far more serious loss to posterity was the house occupied, in 1553, by the Gaoler Nathaniel Partridge. It was in his residence, and in his charge, that Lady Jane Grey lived, dining with the family and enduring her imprisonment with fortitude. These houses, and others nearer the chapel royal now occupied by the chaplain and the doctor, were all rebuilt early in the eighteenth century.

Storms experienced in the Tower are particularly alarming for its residents. At the best of times the 40ft (12m) high walls have a claustrophobic effect, creating a sensation of being at the bottom of a ravine. This impression is heightened during gales, the walls and archways acting like funnels while the wind howls and moans through the arrowslits and round the high turrets. So, primitive reactions can easily be understood as when, on 15 September 1692, a minor earthquake was experienced in the south of England. Although it was felt all over London, little damage was caused. In the Tower's Armoury, racks of lances and swords toppled and crashed to the floor. Suits of armour displayed on dummy figures swayed and rattled violently, with helmets nodding and arms swinging. Little wonder then that the Tower residents were convinced that the Day of Judgement had arrived. Believing that the armoured figures had come alive and were about to march out of the Tower, they took to their heels in panic!

Consternation was also caused whenever explosions, for one motive or another, occurred within the grounds. The one which caused considerable damage to the Middle Tower on 22 November 1548 was accidental, the result of gunpowder being stored there by an underporter. Gunpowder and other munitions were stockpiled in the White Tower for centuries, and a plot discovered in 1593 was obviously intended to make full use of this fact. Two of the conspirators had planned to disguise themselves as labourers and gain access to the White Tower basement. There they would throw balls of slow–burning incendiary material into the gunpowder, the subsequent explosion being powerful enough to demolish the White Tower and most of the surrounding buildings. Before they could put their plan into operation, word reached the Court of Elizabeth, and the men were captured and condemned to death. This, only twelve years before Guy Fawkes and his friends suffered torture in the same tower, and paid the same price.

Many similar plots went wrong through lack of the necessary secrecy, as was the case in October 1615 when yet another attempt was made on the life of James I. Returning to the Tower by river from Gravesend with a hundred or more of his nobles and courtiers, James received warning from an apple-seller on the Wharf that gunpowder ready to be ignited had been hidden in crates where the royal party usually stepped ashore. Landing further along the Wharf, the king's men raised the alarm, catching three of the would-be assassins. Next day, the king addressed a great multitude of his subjects in the fields adjoining the Tower, to assure them of his safety. The culprits, needless to say, were tortured and beheaded. Doubtless the warders on duty at the gates were also punished severely.

A politically motivated explosion which had near fatal results occurred on 24 January 1885, when Irish Fenians detonated bombs in London – two in the Houses of Parliament and one in the Armoury of the White Tower. In those days admission to the Tower was free on Saturdays and so the rooms were crowded with visitors when, at 2pm, the bomb exploded without warning. Windows and doors were instantly blown out and hundreds of rifles crashed from their stands. Thick smoke and dust filled the building, while huge flames roared upwards, setting fire to the ancient timbers of the floor above. The flagstaff at the top of the White Tower was burnt away, and down below, showcases collapsed, showering glass over the panic-stricken victims.

Warders and police worked amongst the burning debris to free the injured, and troops sealed off all exits from the grounds. No one was allowed to leave without being questioned, and in this way the terrorist was identified and later brought to trial. He was found guilty and sentenced to fourteen years' hard labour, not being released until March 1899. No fatalities resulted, and the damage was soon repaired. A new flagpole was later installed and this lasted until 1945 when dry rot necessitated its replacement. A new one was presented by Mr Prentice Bloedel of Vancouver, Canada, on behalf of the boy scouts of British Columbia. A Douglas pine, originally 185ft (56m) tall, was reduced to 85ft (26m) and placed in position in June 1948, since when it has borne the union flag which still flies proudly over the White Tower.

The worst attack on defenceless tourists took place on 17 July 1974. Terrorists placed a bomb beneath a cannon in the basement of the White Tower, the explosion occurring, ironically enough, at just about the same time as that of eighty-nine years earlier. As before, much damage to doors, windows and exhibits was sustained, the blast wrecking showcases and weapons. One woman was killed and nearly forty other visitors injured, many with horrific wounds. Most of them were tourists from abroad, some being young children. Yeoman warders, Tower staff and residents rushed to extricate the trapped casualties. Police, fire brigade and ambulance personnel arrived within minutes and rescue operations got underway. The Tower was closed for several days while repairs were carried out, and now a brass plate set in the floor of the basement marks the site of the atrocity.

Fires of course were always a risk in old buildings, especially in the days prior to the establishment of municipal fire brigades. Leather buckets and hooks to pull down burning thatch were of little use when a city burned, and fortune favoured the Tower in September 1666 when the Great Fire devastated London. The fire started in Pudding Lane, only a few hundred yards west of the Tower, and spread further westwards rapidly, out of control. The country being at war with Holland, the Tower's gunpowder stores were full to overflowing, and it needed little

Yeoman Warders saving the Regalia during the fire of 1841

imagination to visualise the result should the wind change direction. Pepys visited the Tower and climbed on to the high battlements to get a better view of the holocaust, for by then whole areas of the City were in flames, with churches and houses collapsing and making the streets impassable. Within the fortress, warders and soldiers worked nonstop, loading the stocks of gunpowder on to wagons which then ferried them out of danger.

The conflagration spread out in every direction, darkening the sun with a heavy pall of smoke and lighting up the sky at night. Eventually it threatened the Tower as it approached the houses clustered along the Wharf and moat's edge. Charles II visited personally, getting through by boat, and ordered that the houses be demolished to form a fire-break. This measure, and the general direction of the strong winds, saved the Tower of London. The fire burned for five days and left the City a scene of blackened desolation, with over a hundred churches and halls destroyed, and many thousands of houses in ruins.

In the following century, several minor fires occurred within the Tower. New Year's Day 1774 was spoiled for the warders by one that was soon extinguished, causing little damage but much excitement. Another, on 23 July 1788, destroyed an ordnance building, despite the efforts of no fewer than fifteen fire engines to put it out. But these were only forerunners of a major conflagration which started on Saturday night, 30 October 1841, behind the Grand Storehouse. This elegant three-storied building, 370ft (112m) long and 60ft (18m) wide, was everything its name implied, being stacked with sufficient weapons for 60,000 men – field artillery, cannon and mortars. Some rooms displayed tableaux of pistols, bayonets, ceremonial drums and banners; it was a veritable Aladdin's cave of military trophies and equipment.

The fire spread rapidly through the main building, and the castle's alarm bell and the roar of the flames attracted hundreds of Londoners to the edge of the moat to watch the awesome spectacle. So intense was the heat that the lead gutters on the White Tower opposite the Storehouse started to melt, and then a new danger threatened.

Only yards away stood the Martin Tower, at that time the Jewel House. While troops and the recently formed fire brigades fought the fire, Yeoman Warder John Lund and his colleagues, together with the police, rushed to the assistance of

Mr Lenthal Swifte, the Jewel House keeper, in his attempts to remove the regalia to a place of safety. They were hampered by the fact that, to ensure the security of the jewels, the only keys to their protective cage were held by the Lord Chamberlain. The warders and police had therefore to attack the bars with axes and crowbars, desperately levering them apart until an opening was forced wide enough to allow Police Superintendent Pierse to squeeze through. Once in the cage, he passed the precious pieces out to the waiting warders, the smoke making them choke and the intense heat scorching their uniforms. Just in time the last valuable crown was removed and locked up with the others in the Queen's House.

The Grand Storehouse, ablaze from end to end, took nine hours to bring under control, smoke wreathing around the Tower's turrets and the glow illuminating walls and battlements. By dawn little of value was left amidst the charred timbers and smouldering ruins of the devastated building. The scene was described graphically by an eye witness as 'a melancholy sight of awe and wonder, with bayonet points bristling up everywhere, close set and countless, like long blades of grass among the ashes' (Sutherland Gower, page 144).

Rebuilding took place without delay, and two badly damaged towers, the Brick and the Bowyer, were extensively reconstructed. On the site of the Storehouse rose the Waterloo Barracks, now renamed the Waterloo Block and big enough to house a thousand men. A new Jewel House was built, with its keys rather more accessible, and new arms and military equipment replaced those burnt. One can only lament the loss of such irreplaceable items as the torture rack, the wheel of Nelson's ship *Victory*, a drum major's chariot of state, priceless suits of armour, historic Scottish swords, Battle of Waterloo relics, and trophies of William III and General Wolfe.

But the Tower of London, like the unquenchable spirit of the nation, seems to survive all calamities and disasters. Long may it continue to do so.

11 Ghosts!

In the sunlight 'tis easy to swagger and strut
To push on a door that is carelessly shut.
But evening will bring just the hint of a query
Turning reason awry and producing an eerie
Dominion of doubt where once certainty stood –
*   What lies just beyond that great portal of wood?*
Is it fiercesome or gentle? – rapid or slow?
Wilt thou brazenly enter – or tarry – or go?
*   I'll not wait for thine answer*
*   But meet thee below ...!*

You can, if you wish, say they don't exist. However, things happen in the Tower which cannot be explained away, and which were reported, moreover, by responsible, trained observers – yeoman warders, guards and sentries on patrol. After all, why shouldn't events, sad or otherwise, impress themselves on an atmosphere so that their images are still 'visible' centuries later, like ink on blotting paper? And if those events gave rise to highly charged emotions at the time, could not the moans, the screams, the footsteps, continue to echo down the ages?

After the publication of my book on the Tower's ghosts, I received many new reports of supernatural happenings, a few of which I include here. I make no attempt to explain them; I am a retired yeoman warder, not a psychic investigator! Interestingly enough, the visitations don't always restrict themselves to the traditional 'haunting' times after dark. This is fortuitous, allowing the witness to observe details – if not too unnerved!

Events which occurred in the presence of more than one person were related to me by Mr George Trott, who lived for some time in the Martin Tower. This tower once housed the Crown Jewels and was the scene of the attempted robbery by Colonel Blood in 1671, and supernatural happenings were reported there in the last century. Mr Trott took up residence, with his father and mother, in 1921; and from there he relates

My father, mother and I moved into the top living quarter of the Martin Tower, taking it over from yeoman warder Smoker and his wife. They told us they had heard footsteps coming up the inside stairs to the top quarter but when they opened the door there was never anyone there.

Yeoman warder Curtis VC and his wife lived in the downstairs quarter and next day they took us all over the Martin Tower and told us about the footsteps so my mother told me not to be alarmed about it. When my cousin came to live with us she told him the same.

After about five days or so we had just settled down for an evening meal when we heard footsteps so my father thought it was Mr Curtis or his wife and he opened the door of the kitchen/living room and there was no one there. The footsteps stopped. We carried on with our meal and later I went to bed.

Now about the second Sunday night we heard the footsteps and they came up to the door – and the door opened – but there was nobody there! My mother looked out and my father checked the downstairs doors which were locked, including the door leading to the battlements. The door between the downstairs and upstairs was also locked. Dad called yeoman warder Curtis and told him about it and he said 'So you've had your visitor – it won't be long before you hear the footsteps again!'.

Dad got the foreman of the Ministry of Works to check the door and had a lock which had a sliding catch fitted underneath. Meanwhile Dad had told Sir George (Keeper of the Jewels) and Lady Younghusband and she visited mother and had a good talk. She said she had a friend in Cambridge who was interested in such 'goings on' as she called them.

Later on the footsteps came up the stairs again. Dad had locked the door and put the catch on. The footsteps stopped – and the door opened! The lock and catch were still in the locked position, we were amazed! Dad looked round the Tower again, everything was secure, so he relocked the door.

About the third week in November 1921, Lady Younghusband brought two gentlemen with her and introduced them to us. They also met Mr and Mrs Curtis, and then they

checked the tower from top to bottom. They also looked up
the history of the Martin Tower.

My mother said that next time the door opened she would
say 'Come in Mary' and tell me to shut the door.

Nothing happened for a few days, until the last Sunday in
November. One of the gentlemen was with us, and he took
Dad and Mr Curtis with him when he locked the two main
doors and the side doors to the tower, and the door between
the upstairs and downstairs. We settled down for a late meal
about 7.45pm (I was allowed to stay up on Sundays).

Mother was at the stove, I was reading, Dad and the
gentleman were talking – when the footsteps came up the
stairs!

The door was locked and the bottom catch on. The
footsteps stopped – and the door opened! My mother said
'Come in, Mary – close the door, George!'. But the gentleman said 'No, stay still'. He looked at a thermometer and two
more instruments and took readings. He then went with Dad
and checked all doors, which were found still locked. They
went to the top of the tower, all secure.

We all settled down after that, and I went to bed while they
had a drink and a chat. Sir George and Lady Younghusband
came over, and a report was sent to the Resident Governor.

When my cousin came to live with us he soon got used to
the footsteps and door opening; they wanted to change the
door but my mother said leave it, as she was quite happy with
'Mary calling'. She said the footsteps were light so it must be a
lady calling.

Later we moved out, and the Ministry of Works' officers
took over. One of the staff called on mother and told her that
he had heard more than once footsteps coming up the stairs and
stopping outside, and when he called out 'Come in' nobody
came, and no one was there. My mother told him to tell
everyone else not to worry, it was only Mary calling.

By a strange coincidence another holder of the Victoria Cross,
Britain's highest award for bravery, was also involved in an eerie
occurrence on the other side of the Tower Green in what is now
called the Queen's House. This sixteenth-century dwelling has
housed many historic prisoners, Anne Boleyn, Katherine Howard, Guy Fawkes, William Penn and others, and is the house
of the Resident Governor.

Colonel Burges VC held this post in 1923 and, as related by George Trott, had gone to bed early one night. He was reading, when he heard footsteps come down the corridor and stop outside his bedroom. He thought it was his batman and so told him to come in, but the footsteps carried on down the corridor. The next day he asked his batman about this and was told that he had not been upstairs. Later on the same thing happened again, so the colonel had an alarm switch fitted and when it occurred again, he pressed the button and the soldier on duty below came running up. As he reached the corridor he heard the footsteps moving along ahead of him. The whole house was searched and everything found secure. The yeoman warder on watch duty reported the matter to Chief Warder Smoker, and though it happened again, Colonel Burges never seemed to worry about it.

However, in 1933 he was replaced by Colonel Faviell DSO, who was told about the mysterious footsteps. Some time afterwards his wife, who had forgotten all about the story, was in bed when the footsteps passed her door. She thought it was one of the soldiers visiting her maid, so spoke to her about it. The maid denied it and so Mrs Faviell had the workmen check all the doors and locks. Not only was the alarm switch overhauled, but it was arranged that when Mrs Faviell opened the bedroom door, all the lights along the corridor would come on.

A few nights later, as she lay in bed, the footsteps approached. Getting up, she pressed the alarm switch, alerting the soldier on duty below. He locked the front door and ran up the stairs. Meanwhile, Mrs Faviell had opened the bedroom door flooding the corridor with light – and revealing nothing else, although the footsteps continued along the corridor! Bravely she ran after 'whoever it was' but the footsteps suddenly stopped. More soldiers were summoned and a search was made, but as usual nothing was found.

But all that happened many years ago and could have been creaking floorboards! What about actual sightings, recently? Well, in January 1982, at 4.30am, the yeoman warder on watch was in the Byward Tower. This guardroom has been manned day and night by the warders and their predecessors for over seven hundred years, and the Watchman was the only one on duty at that time. He sat opposite the huge stone fireplace, which now houses a gas-fire. Two electric lights were on, one at

The front cover of a guide book published in 1884

each end of the small guardroom.

Suddenly he became aware of a buzzing sound, like that of a fly. Looking up he saw, not the gas-fire, but a roaring fire of logs or coal. In front of it stood two men, side by side. They both had beards, and he noted their spindly legs, as if they were wearing breeches and stockings. The bright glare of the fire prevented him noticing any details of their dress. They appeared to be talking to each other, and then suddenly one moved his head, to lean forward and stare at the dumbstruck warder! Next minute both men vanished. The gas-fire reappeared, leaving the Watchman to collect his senses and hope for the dawn's early arrival. There is one fascinating point on which to ponder – if the 'man' leant forward and saw the Watchman: who thought who was a ghost?

Before the public are admitted to the grounds, the White Tower staff sweep the floors and prepare for the coming day's rush of tourists. At 8.05 one morning in 1978, a warden thus engaged noticed a woman through one of the tall glass show-cases. Puzzled by a stranger's presence at that time of day, he went towards her, only to see her move through an archway into the next room. Yet when he arrived there it was empty, and the only way out was up a spiral stair to the chapel. He climbed the narrow stairway and reached the heavy oak door to the chapel to find it securely locked, and although a search was carried out, the results were negative.

Another incident in the White Tower occurred in September 1980, when the night security guard was patrolling. It was 11.15pm and the guard was approaching the spiral stairway which connects the vaults with the uppermost floors. As he started to go down, he was aware of a woman to his left, going up. He had taken two steps further down before he realised what he had seen, so he turned and ascended. He found nothing, all doors ahead of him being locked securely, and he had all the keys!

He described later how he had been unable to see the upper half of her body for she had leant forward climbing the steep circular stairs and so was rounding the newel post. However, he distinctly saw that she was wearing a black and grey panelled skirt. Again, a thorough search of the eleventh-century building revealed nothing.

Finally, I include an experience that was recounted to me by a gentleman who would prefer to be known by the initials JHW. Although somewhat unnerved at the time, his profession re-quired him to have an eye for detail, coupled with a photo-graphic recall of memory. I quote the report in his own words to preserve spontaneity.

Though I have passed by the rear of the Tower hundreds of times, this was the only time I felt or saw anything. It was 7.30am on 11 March 1980, a slightly misty morning. As I was approaching Traitors' Gate I noticed a blue light which was flickering and therefore drew my attention.

On looking down I was amazed to see a group of people in what appeared to be Tudor dress. There were about eight or more of them. Leading the procession was a very big man dressed in a leather apron, closely followed by two men carrying pikes or something like that, then two more men very well dressed. They wore red velvet with gold thread or brocade, and one had a small ruff, also a lace collar under the ruff. One seemed to be red headed and had a small beard, the other dark, no hat, and a small beard, his costume came up to his neck, no ruff, long puffed sleeves and several rings on his fingers. One man had a long gold chain.

Behind them were two women in their early twenties, both very richly clothed. One seemed to be dressed in grey material, silk and brocaded, with a low neckline. Both women had a small tiara, what appeared to be rows of pearls shaped like a crescent on the crown of their heads. The other woman's dress was of a brownish colour. Both had necklets of pearls, double loops, also a golden chain and pendant of some sort, long sleeves but without frills. The hair of one was sort of auburn, the other brown. Both dresses were studded with pearls, diamonds, etc, and gold thread or something like it.

The woman in brown was holding a box against her chest with both hands. It was quite a small box, more of a casket than a box. The woman in grey was clasping a prayer book with a cross on it.

Following them were two more men carrying pikes. They were dressed the same as the other pikemen, with black hats and capes or cloaks.

The figures seemed to be gliding along as in a boat on the water, and the blue light was above them and seemed to move with the figures, growing fainter all the time they were in view.

The impression only lasted about a minute or two, then there was some movement along the wharf and they all vanished like a puff of smoke.

I cannot say if what I saw was real or not, but I can assure you I don't want to see it again, for it left me feeling greatly puzzled and feeling a great deal of sadness, also very cold. I have had many sleepless nights since then, it is a welcome to have happened in daylight and not at night which could have had a disastrous effect. However, at no time did I feel any menacing or evil feeling towards me, only as I have already said, a feeling of overwhelming sadness and coldness.

As well as being an observer, I felt that someone or something was also observing me, to what purpose one cannot tell. In my case there was no fear, but a knowledge that I was privileged to see it. I can only say once more I hope never to see anything like it anymore.

So don't think that supernatural happenings occur only at night, to guards and warders. Once you are in the grounds of the Tower, at any time of the day, you are just as likely to sense a touch on the shoulder, half see a shape rounding the corner, perhaps hear the echoes of a stifled scream ...

After all, why should *you* be exempt?

Conclusion

A yeoman warder's life, then, is full, hard working and quite unique, a crazy mixture of tradition and modernity. Up to his knees in history and soft-drink cans, he lives near the Crown Jewels in a castle on the no 15 London bus route.

Sometimes he wears a tee shirt, other times an Elizabethan ruff. He can carry an 8ft (2.4m) long partizan inside the Tower, but would be arrested if found with a flick-knife outside. His working hours are spent in the public glare, whether on duty at the gate at 6.30 on a winter's morning, or conducting two hundred tourists around on a summer afternoon. His time is filled with crowds and queues, cameras and questions, ceremonies and state events, and if tempers get a little strained after coping with up to 12,000 visitors a day, he is after all a human being and not a cardboard cut-out.

Known and respected all over the world, the Yeoman Warders' standards are high, their dedication unquestioned. Applaud them, for they represent the glories and traditions of England.

Appendix

The Warder's Oath as sworn on 11 October 1727

You shall Swear to serve the High and Mighty Prince George, by the grace of God King of England Scotland France and Ireland, Defender of the Faith, and his Heirs and Successors Lawful Kings or Queens of this Realm, both faithfully and truly in the office that you are now calld unto, that is, to be an ordinary Yeoman Warder of the Tower of London, and in all things touching his honour and safety, you shall neither your Selfe do, procure or give consent to be done, anything that shall be prejudicial to his Majestys Person, State or honour.

And if you shall hear or understand of any bodily hurt, dishonour or prejudice to his Majesty or any of the Royal Family, or to the Tower of London, you shall do as much as in you ly's to hinder the same, or to disclose to the Kings Majesty or to such of his Privey Councill or your Commanding Officer as you may best come unto, and by all wais and means you can to make the same truly to be known. Moreover you shall serve no man for wages, livery or fee, without the consent of his Majesty or his Councill.

You shall be obedient to the Chief Governour of the Tower, your Captain, and also such officers there as are to have the Command over you in the Tower. You shall not depart or absent your selfe from your service in the Tower into the country without the licence of the Chief Governour or other Commanding Officer. You shall keep his Majestys Peace yourself in the Tower and in all other places, and see the same kept by others as much as in you lyeth.

Warder's Reply: All these things I will well and truly do, observe and keep, so help me God and the contents of this Bible.

Acknowledgements

To my wife Shelagh who, when not researching little known facts for this book, renovated my ruff, polished my partizan and brushed my Tudor bonnet.

Further acknowledgements to Mr G. D. Trott for his invaluable reminiscences.

Bibliography

Abbott, G. *Ghosts of the Tower of London* (Heinemann, 1980)
  Great Escapes from the Tower of London (Heinemann, 1982)
Ainsworth, W. H. *Tower of London* (R. Bentley, 1850)
Bayley, J. *History of the Tower* (Jennings and Chaplin, 1830)
Bell, D. C. *Chapel in the Tower* (John Murray, 1877)
Bennett, E. *Tower Menagerie* (1829)
British Library. Tower of London Records, State Papers and Documents
Britton and Brayley. *Memoirs of the Tower of London* (1830)
Dixon, Hepworth. *Her Majesty's Tower* (Bickers and Son, 1885)
Fox, C. *General Williamson's Diary* (Campden Society, 1912)
Francis, René. *Story of the Tower of London* (George G. Harrap & Co, 1910)
Harper, C. G. *Tower of London* (Chapman and Hall, 1909)
Penny Magazine Supplements (1836)
Preston, T. *Yeomen of the Guard* (Harrison and Sons, 1885)
de Ros, Lord. *Tower of London* (John Murray, 1866)
Sutherland Gower, Lord. *Tower of London* (G. Bell & Son, 1901)
Thornbury, W. *Old & New London* (Cassell, Petter & Galpin, 1873)
Younghusband, Sir George. *Tower of London from Within* (Herbert Jenkins Ltd, 1919)

Other David & Charles books on London

WALKING LONDON'S WATERWAYS
Bryan Fairfax

The most satisfying way of exploring the fascinating waterways of the London area, and of escaping from the hustle and bustle of city life, is on foot; and this book gives full instructions for seventeen varied walks, with detailed information on relevant maps, public transport, and starting and stopping places. Each walk is accompanied by clear maps, and all are accessible from main rail and bus routes. Every Londoner (and London visitor) should have this book.

COUNTRY WALKS AROUND LONDON
Leigh Hatts

This book is an ideal companion for those living in and around London who would like to get out of the city for a change of scenery. The walks cover all the Home Counties as well as the London Boroughs and offer the reader the chance to explore his or her surrounding environment. They are linked with bus, tubes or BR's suburban network.
'For those living or holidaying in the capital this book is a revelation.'— *Woman's Weekly*
'Plenty of interesting historical information is included and the walk descriptions are carefully done.'—*Great Outdoors*

THE MAN WHO BUILT LONDON TRANSPORT
A Biography of Frank Pick
Christian Barman

Here is the story of the remarkable man who steered the city's transport system from the early days of the Underground through to World War II. His efforts produced much that is familiar today – the circular symbol on bus stops, the tradition of fine design in London Transport posters, the light and spacious stations of Charles Holden – as well as a rational, efficient service and a clean and orderly environment for travellers. In his hands London Transport became, in the words of *The Times*, a 'civilising agency'.
'What the book does splendidly is to give us an insight into Pick the man, the artist and the administrator... This is a book to be recommended without hesitation.'—*Modern Railways*

LONDON AND ITS RAILWAYS
R. Davies and M. D. Grant

In *London and its Railways* the authors discuss in twelve thematic chapters the history and development of London's railways, not forgetting the social and economic reasons for their construction, and sometimes closure, with numerous maps and more than 120 photographs showing the capital's railways past and present. They look at passenger services for business and pleasure, the great terminus stations, main lines, freight, the docks, depots, and lines of which hardly a trace remains, and surprisingly despite much standardisation many unique aspects of the past still show through.
'... an excellent introduction to London's railways...'—*Journal of the Railway and Canal Historical Society*